SOCIAL SALVATION

BY

WASHINGTON GLADDEN

Wipf & Stock
PUBLISHERS
Eugene, Oregon

Wipf and Stock Publishers
199 West 8th Avenue, Suite 3
Eugene, Oregon 97401

Social Salvation
By Gladden, Washington
ISBN: 1-59244-556-X
Publication date 2/16/2004
Previously published by Houghton Mifflin, 1902

Published April, 1902.

PREFACE

THE following lectures have been prepared for delivery, in March, 1902, before the students of the Divinity School of Yale University, upon the Lyman Beecher Foundation. This preface is written before the date of their delivery, but if no accidents shall occur, what is here printed will have been spoken before it is published.

Fifteen years ago last month I had the honor of speaking in the same place upon the same foundation. That course of lectures upon the relation of the pulpit to the social questions of the day was afterwards printed under the title, "Tools and the Man: Property and Industry under the Christian Law." In the present course economic questions have therefore been passed by, and attention has been drawn to other problems with which the Christian pulpit has need to concern itself. That the Christian pulpit recognizes this need I have some means of knowing, for scarcely a day passes that does not bring me letters from ministers of the gospel asking for suggestions and helps in the study of some of the questions with which these lectures deal. It is quite impossible for me to answer these inquiries, but I hope that this volume may afford some assistance to those who seek such direction.

The lectures are addressed to men who are preparing for the ministry, but the truth presented is not for ministers alone. The whole discussion concerns laymen as deeply as ministers; the subjects discussed bring home to every citizen his responsibilities. Ministers are not in this book considered as possessing any priestly character; they are spoken to as men who by their intelligence and their social position ought to be leaders of public opinion; the remedies for social ills here suggested are not ecclesiastical remedies, they are such as require the coöperation of all men of good-will in every community. And yet I hope that those who read the book will be able to recognize the significance of its title. If Society were articulate, its cry would be, "What must I do to be saved?" That is the social question which this volume tries to answer. How incomplete and fragmentary the answer is, no one knows so well as I: but it is such as I have, and I give it in the hope that its broken lights may lead some who read it into larger vision.

WASHINGTON GLADDEN.

FIRST CONGREGATIONAL CHURCH,
 COLUMBUS, O., February 25, 1902.

CONTENTS

CHAP.		PAGE
I.	Religion and the Social Question	1
II.	The Care of the Poor	32
III.	The State and the Unemployed	61
IV.	Our Brothers in Bonds	94
V.	Social Vices	135
VI.	Public Education	172
VII.	The Redemption of the City	203
	References and Suggestions	237

SOCIAL SALVATION

I

RELIGION AND THE SOCIAL QUESTION

WE are to consider, in the hours which we shall spend together, the relation of the Christian Church and the Christian Pastor to Current Social Questions. Of what are commonly known as the Social Questions, the one which stands foremost is the industrial question, the question of the organization and remuneration of labor; the relation of employers and employees; the problem of the distribution of the product of industry. To that question I gave consideration in a course of lectures delivered several years ago, in this place. I shall not, therefore, dwell upon it at this time. To ignore it will not, indeed, be possible; for all the other questions which we are to consider have their economic aspects, and cannot be adequately treated without constant reference to industrial conditions. "The question of food and clothes," says Charles Ferguson, "is inextricably bound up with the interests of arts and letters, and all together are meshed and woven in with the grand eternal issues, so that we cannot make an inch of progress in the settlement of economic questions save as we make progress in the settlement of the other questions."[1] The converse is equally true. The wage-worker's problems will, however, be before us, in these studies, only incidentally; we shall be chiefly occupied with other phases of the manifold inquiry with which society, in this day and generation, is exploring its own doings and misdoings.

The fact that there is a social question is a hopeful symptom. It springs from some dim recognition of the solidarity of society, — of the fact that we are members one of another; that the ills which the community is heir to are matters of concern to all of us. It is not alone the sociologists and the philanthropists who are aware of the existence of social questions; in a more or less definite way we are all thinking about them.

It is involved in what I have said that the social question, as a whole, presents itself to our minds as a pathological study. If we are not

[1] *The Religion of Democracy*, p. 66. The correlation of the social questions is admirably shown in the last chapter of Professor F. G. Peabody's *Jesus Christ and the Social Question*.

quite as hopeless as Isaiah was when he cried
out to Jerusalem: "The whole head is sick, and
the whole heart faint; from the sole of the foot
even unto the head there is no soundness in it;
but wounds, and bruises, and putrefying sores,"
— we are still painfully conscious that there are
morbid conditions in modern society, tendencies to decay, ills that call for healing. The
shapes that rise up before us in these searchings
of heart are poverty and pauperism, idleness
and intemperance, bankrupt households and
neglected children, groups of incapables and
ne'er-do-weels and criminals, — the multitudes
on whom Jesus looked with compassion because
they were distressed and scattered as sheep not
having a shepherd. It is through his eyes that
we are looking upon the suffering and misery
that surround us; the social question springs
from the compassion with which he has touched
our hearts.

It is true that the pathological study of society leads directly to questions of social organization; in the face of so much poverty and
suffering we are constrained to ask ourselves
whether something is not wrong with the social
framework; whether reconstruction rather than
repairs is not the thing most needed. "The
social question of the present age," says Professor Peabody, "is not a question of mitigating

the evils of the existing order, but a question whether the existing order itself shall last. It is not so much a problem of social amelioration which occupies the modern mind as a problem of social transformation and reconstruction. The new social interest is concerned not so much with effects as with causes; not with social therapeutics, but with social bacteriology and hygiene. Indeed, in this frame of mind there is often to be discerned a violent reaction from traditional ways of charity and from moderate measures of reform. The time is wasted, it is urged, which is given to lopping off occasional branches of social wrong, when the real social question cuts at the root from which these branches grow. Instead of inquiring what ways of charity are wise, let us rather, it is urged, inquire why charity is necessary, and why poverty exists."[1] In these words Professor Peabody is stating the social question not as it presents itself to his own mind, but rather as it takes form in the minds of the more radical reformers. We may not take their point of view, but we must admit that the question they raise is pertinent. There are reasons for believing that the social ailments are constitutional, rather than local, and that the remedies must reach the seat of the disorder. But if the analogy

[1] *Jesus Christ and the Social Question*, p. 5.

which we have been following is of any significance, — if society possesses any of the characteristics of an organism, — the remedies which are truly radical will not be those which are generally contemplated by reformers who call themselves radicals. If a house has fallen into decay, the best thing to do may be to pull it down and build on a new foundation, with all the modern improvements. Reconstruction, rather than repair, may, in that case, be the best policy. But if a tree is pining, it cannot be treated after that fashion. It may need pruning, and its life may need invigorating by the addition of fertilizers to the soil in which it grows: it cannot be pulled down and rebuilt. The same is true of a human body. If there is serious disease, the physician seeks to allay suffering and to hold in check the morbid tendencies while he reinforces at every point the vital energies. When the cure is complete, it is evident that no reconstruction has taken place; it is the same body, with the same parts and organs, fulfilling the same functions as before.

I am aware that analogies are not proofs, and I would not put too much weight on this one; but it is certain that society much more nearly resembles a tree or a human body than a house; it is a living thing; it has some of the characteristics of a physical organism, and we shall come nearer to the truth if we apply to it the laws of biology than if we try to deal with it under the laws of mechanics. That is a truth which all radical reformers should consider well. Society cannot be pulled down and rebuilt successfully. It must keep on growing out of its own roots; its vital processes can never be suspended. Morbid tendencies may be arrested; its life may be replenished; possibly its vital forces may be directed into new channels, but the structural principles must remain essentially the same. The one lesson that the social reformer as well as the theological reformer needs to learn is the lesson of evolution.

We shall get a little nearer to the heart of the social question when we begin to ask whether the answer to it is to come through the individual, or through the social organization. Where shall the remedy be applied? Is it the men and women who most need healing and restoration, or is it the society in which they live? The theory of Orthodox Protestantism puts the whole emphasis upon the individual; it has no hope of saving society except as it saves the souls of individual men and women. Unquestionably its tendency has been to overstate the importance of the individual and to ignore the "organic filaments" by which a man is vitally bound to the community. It is the belief of most preachers of the gospel that if all the men and women in the community were "soundly converted," there would be no social question. If the term "soundly converted" be made broad enough, that may be true. But the truth must be confessed that multitudes of those who answer all the requirements of the ordinary evangelical experience; who are known in their churches as men and women of deep and devoted piety; who, in the charitable judgment of their neighbors, have sincerely repented of their sins, and accepted of the divine forgiveness, and consecrated their lives to the service of God, and are prayerfully endeavoring to do his will, — multitudes, I say, of such as these are so far from helping to solve the social question that they are doing a great deal to make it insolvable by deepening the antipathies and alienations which weaken the social bond. The trouble with them is that they have been converted as individuals; religion is with them too much an individual matter between themselves and God. The fact that one man can no more be a Christian alone than one man can sing an oratorio alone is the fact which they have not clearly comprehended. The failure to realize this truth results in highly unsocial conduct on the part of many whose piety is unquestioned. I could easily multiply instances which have come under my own observation of men and women who were humble, trustful, prayerful; who obeyed, also, all the ordinary rules of morality, — being chaste, truthful, honest, and bountiful in their gifts, — and yet who were deeply distrusted and even cordially hated by those who knew them best. Shall we say that it was their superior goodness that repelled their neighbors? That is not a safe theory. Shall we say that they were hypocrites? God forbid that we should thus judge them. Their defective conduct arose from their failure to comprehend their vital relations to their fellow men. That the essence of religion is righteousness they would not deny, but the social nature of righteousness they do not understand. The breadth and comprehensiveness of the law of love has not been brought home to them. They think of God as a Moral Governor, and conceive of his kingdom in this world as the maintenance of a certain rectoral justice between man and man; those, therefore, who keep well within the requirements of common honesty are not transgressors, and have nothing to repent of. Within those requirements there is room for a great deal of indifference and hard-hearted disregard for the welfare of our neighbors. And I think that those who scrupulously keep to the letter of their contracts, who always pay their debts, who can never be accused of misrepresentation or fraud, but who, standing on these principles of common honesty, push their advantages relentlessly, and are willing to profit by the misfortune or the ignorance of those with whom they deal, are rather worse hated, in their generation, than the recognized sharpers and swindlers. This may seem a hard judgment, but there is a profound reason for it. For the conception of the divine Fatherhood, which has been gaining possession of the mind of Christendom, has greatly modified our ideas of obligation and sin, and our ideals of character. The discord between the selfish soul and the Father whose name is love is seen to be a far more serious thing than disobedience to a Moral Governor whose reign consists in the maintenance of rectoral righteousness. The same insight shows us what is the root of all the trouble between ourselves and our fellow men. "The huge disease of society," says Dr. Horton, "is caused by the *lovelessness* of men," — not by their dishonesty or their perfidy. When we realize that the essence of sin is the defect of love, there is a new standard of judgment by which to measure human character, and there are many who fall before it. The trouble with these pious folk who have incurred the ill-will of their neighbors is simply this, — that they have kept the whole law, as the Pharisees kept it, and yet have offended at one point, as the Pharisees offended, — that one point being precisely the vital point, in which the whole Christian morality originates. What they lack is simply the love which is the fulfilling of the law. Their Christian experience is, therefore, radically defective, because they have had no due sense of sin and have never thoroughly repented. And the reason of this is found in the failure to bring home to them the truth concerning their social relations. They have practically ignored their most fundamental obligation, because they have not conceived of Christian experience as involving social relations.

The social question, as it now presents itself, — the social injustice and disorder and discontent are due, in my judgment, very largely to the lack of clearness in the minds of Christian people at this very point. Not many of them have yet fully comprehended the fact that the law of love governs the whole of life; that it defines our relations to men not only in the home and in the church, but in industry and commerce and politics. Many of them flatly deny that the law of love can be applied to the ordinary social relations; most of them make but feeble attempts to rule their lives by it, in the larger realms of human activity. When we say, therefore, that if all men were "soundly converted" there would be no social question, we must bear in mind the fact that no man can be said to be soundly converted who fails to understand or to obey the law of love. Conversion is something more than a change in the religious sentiments; it involves a change in the ruling ideas as well as in the sensibilities. "Change your minds!" is the first order. This means that there is a system of relations in which you with all other beings are included; the fundamental trouble with you is that you are out of your place in that system, and that you have wrong ideas about it all; you must get right ideas, and through right ideas you must get into right relations. Salvation is just that — getting into right relations; and no man is in the way of salvation until he has in some dim way grasped that idea, and tried to realize it.

It is clear, then, that the view of the Christian life which puts the whole emphasis upon individual experience is seen to result in defective conduct and in morbid social conditions. And I have no doubt that the defective conduct of which we have spoken, and the unhappy social conditions which have resulted therefrom, have been due in considerable measure to an excessive emphasis upon individual experience, and a failure to give proper weight to the social relations and obligations, in the fulfillment of which alone the Christian life can find expression.

It may be said that the defects which I have pointed out are, after all, only the defects of individuals, and can be remedied only by the action of individuals. This is true; but the defective conduct of these individuals is *in their social relations.* Their defective conduct cannot be remedied unless they have the right ideas as well as the right feelings about their social relations. The social ideal, as well as the individual ideal, must be clearly before their minds; indeed, the two can no more be separated in Christian morality than the outside of a curve can be separated from the inside. The morality which separates them is something other than Christian morality. No individual can be right with his God who is not in right relations to his neighbors. And it is doubtful whether any individual can have any adequate idea of his relation to God except as he learns it in the fulfillment of his relations to his fellow men. "He that loveth not his brother whom he hath seen, cannot love God whom he hath not seen."

"Belief in God," says President Hyde, "is something no logician can argue into us, no apologist can prove; any more than by arguing the logician can satisfy our hunger if we have no food, or the apologist can assuage our thirst if we refuse to drink the water that he offers. The bread and the water of the spiritual life are the doing of one's duty and the service of our fellows; and without these elements one can never have the life of fellowship with God, of which they are the indispensable constituents. Faith in a living God, in other words, must be wrought out of our own moral and spiritual experience. The man who gains it in that way, by doing his work as a member of a great spiritual order, and serving his fellow men as members of the same great kingdom of which he is a part, comes to know God with the same certainty that the fish knows the water, the bird the air, or any living thing the environment in which it lives and moves and has its being." [1]

It is this spiritual order through which God is revealed to man, and through which man approaches God. There can be no adequate knowledge of God save that which is mediated through this spiritual order which is the social order.

All these considerations seem to make it plain that there is no possibility of separating the individual from society, and drawing a line between individual experience and social responsi-

[1] *God's Education of Man*, p. 22.

bility. A great economist has said that in the modern industrial world there is, in strictness, no such thing as an individual; and if this is true of economics, it cannot be less true of ethics and religion. When the fundamental fact of theology is the fact of fatherhood, the fact of brotherhood cannot be ignored in any phase of religious experience.

Any treatment of social questions which failed to bring the responsibility for right social actions home to individuals would, indeed, be defective treatment; on the other hand, any discussion of the problems of the individual life which did not keep the social environment steadily in view would be utterly inadequate.

I am therefore unable to understand how Christianity, whether as a law or as a gospel, can be intelligently or adequately preached or lived in these days without a constant reference to social questions. No individual is soundly converted until he comprehends his social relations and strives to fulfill them; and the work of growth and sanctification largely consists in a clearer apprehension of these relations and a more earnest effort to fill them with the life of the divine Spirit. The kingdom of heaven is *within* us and *among* us; the preposition, in Christ's saying, seems to have the double meaning. It cannot be among us unless it is within us, and it cannot be within us without being among us.

It would seem, therefore, that the minister's work, in these days, must lie, very largely, along the lines of social amelioration. He is bound to understand the laws of social structure. It is just as needful that he should understand the constitution of human society as that he should understand the constitution of the human soul; the one comes under his purview no less directly than the other. He does not know definitely what sin is, unless he understands the nature of the social bond; he does not surely know what salvation means until he has comprehended the reciprocal action of society upon the individual and of the individual upon society. The men who are working out their own salvation are doing it largely through the establishment of right relations between themselves and their neighbors, and he cannot help them in this unless he has some clear idea of what these right relations are.

I am aware that there have been good men to whom these social aspects of the work of the ministry did not strongly appeal. Our own Dr. Dale of Birmingham, England, was one of the wisest and strongest of our Congregational ministers; and he was inclined to deprecate all attempts to unite social enterprises with the work of the church. To what extent he preached on such subjects I do not know, — I think not often; and he did not approve of enlisting the church, as such, in schemes of social amelioration. He thought the church ought to be inspired, from the pulpit, with the enthusiasm of humanity, which would lead its members to engage actively in social service; but he did not consider the church itself a fitting instrument for such service. Dr. Dale himself was a most active and zealous worker in many social reforms; he was a member of the great national commission by which the present system of public primary education was organized; he was recognized as one of the most influential leaders of the Liberal Party; he was one of the foremost citizens of Birmingham. His conduct shows, therefore, what relation he thought a Christian man and a Christian minister ought to sustain to current social questions. All that he intended to discountenance was the enlistment of the church in this kind of service. These are his words. He is speaking of the contention that the church should interest itself in social questions: —

"If all that is meant is that Christian men as citizens should do their utmost to improve the social and economic condition of the people, there is nothing new in the proposal. For thirty years I have been preaching that doctrine, and according to my strength and light have been endeavoring to practice it. Nor have Christian men generally been indifferent to the duty. In the agitation which secured the great though imperfect Education Act of 1870, — an Act which has achieved an immense improvement in the condition of great masses of the people, — a large proportion of the men who did most of the work, and who encountered most of the obloquy which has to be endured by all reformers, were ministers and members of churches in Birmingham and other parts of England. But we did our work as citizens. Our churches, as I remember, were not asked to pass resolutions in favor of a system of education, 'national, compulsory, unsectarian, and free,' nor did we make collections for the League. I believe that the work was best done in that way. The church should create in all its members an eager desire to lessen the sorrow, the suffering, and the injustice as well as the sin of the world; but it is not yet clear to my mind that the church, as a religious society, should take part in political, social, and economic agitation."[1]

There is, indeed, some good reason for doubting whether local churches should turn them-

[1] The International Congregational Council, London, 1891, *Authorized Record of Proceedings*, pp. xxxi, xxxii.

selves into clubs for any sort of political or social propagandism; these are questions upon which there are apt to be differences of opinion, and a church would better not undertake any kind of active work in which its members cannot pretty unanimously agree. It is doubtless better that organizations should be formed outside the churches, bringing together men of good-will from all the churches, for the promotion of temperance, and municipal reform, and other general social interests. These movements, as Dr. Dale suggests, the churches should inspire, and the members of the churches will do a considerable portion of their Christian work in them.

But how is the church to "create in its members an eager desire to lessen the sorrow, the suffering, and the injustice as well as the sin of the world?" Can this be done by purely abstract teaching? Must not the church encourage its minister to keep it well informed respecting these conditions? Must not the pulpit, in wise proportion, set forth the law of love, as it applies to the institutions and the customs of society, and show what evils result from its violation, and what blessings flow from obeying it? I do not understand how the church can inspire its members to perform their social duties, unless the church is thoroughly interested in the whole subject, and feels that its religion is vain, if it be not pouring a stream of saving influence into all the various channels of social activity.

I find in an essay by one of the most thoughtful and judicious of modern writers another warning against the kind of preaching which I am advocating, to which I desire to draw your attention: —

"To what extent is the Christianity preached to be an applied Christianity? In what way and to what extent are the social, the economical, and the political questions of the hour to be dealt with by the preacher? Apostolic Christianity offers an answer which it were well if our own day would carefully restudy. We find in the primitive church a complete absence of what may be called the ordinary social, economical, and political propaganda. The conditions in these respects were in all conscience bad enough, but they did not form the subject of Christ's or the apostles' preaching. Slavery existed, and in the most cruel form, but no anti-slavery crusade was set afoot. Judea was a crushed nationality, but these Jewish exhorters had nothing to say about a political redemption. One saw everywhere the extremest poverty, but the disciples never interested themselves in the principles of 'The Wealth of Nations.' Why was this? The lesson has been strangely misunderstood, and by more than one side. In some quarters the facts are used to show the utter impracticability of Christianity as a system of life; in others to show that the only true follower of Christ is the self-renouncing monk. Both are wrong. The reason why primitive Christianity had no specific anti-slavery, anti-poverty, anti-despotism propaganda lay in no sense in the fact that it acquiesced in slavery or poverty or despotism. Actually it was the enemy of them all, and in the end will be fatal to them all. The primitive silence on these matters lay in the fact to which we need to-day to give our fullest attention, that the new thing which Christianity had brought in was of infinitely more value to life than all these, and its propagation accordingly of far more importance. If only the pulpit would believe it! When the preacher has become merely political, it is because he has lost grip of religion. As long as this last is vital in him, he cannot help seeing that it is of infinitely more political and social and economical value than any politics or socialisms or economics. To Paul it was so much more worth while to make a slave a Christian than to agitate for his freedom! There will always be enough and to spare of politicians; what the world really wants is men who have news from the land of the ideal, who have God's life within them, who open afresh the springs of living water that quench the thirst of the soul."[1]

I have quoted at length this impressive protest, because it is the strongest statement I have read of the objection we are considering. We shall all do well to give earnest heed to it.

One point of the argument is familiar, but it has less force than is sometimes supposed. The fact that Jesus and his apostles did not deal with social questions in their political aspects may be explained by the fact that those to whom they spoke had no political responsibilities. They were not citizens, they were subjects; to preach politics to them would be like preaching about dancing to people with amputated limbs. If the followers of Jesus had been sovereigns, men clothed with political responsibility, probably he would have had something to say to them about their political duties. The men to whom you and I preach are sovereigns, — the sovereign people; voters in this country are "the powers that be;" they are ordained of God to organize and administer civil society, and they need instruction about their duties. The affirmative considerations which this writer urges are, however, of deep significance, as we

[1] Rev. J. Brierley, in London *Christian World*, July 25, 1901.

shall presently see. Nor am I sure that he would not assent to most of what I have been trying to urge. A little further on in the same essay I find him saying this: —

"That the church is the representative of the eternal in the midst of time does not, however, absolve it from a heavy responsibility in relation to the things of time. Its message will have these continually within its scope, but ever to bring them under its own light, to view them *sub specie æternitatis*. The pulpit cannot be silent on sins, whether national or individual, that are destroying spiritual life; no, not though it suffers as did a Chrysostom at Constantinople or a Savonarola at Florence. But when men speak on these themes, they must have a call. The true prophet knows that his message has been given to him, and that it must be spoken at all hazards. The question of pulpit speech or silence on a given theme depends so much on *who* is in the pulpit. No man should speak on disputed points who has not first earned the right to speak; a right centred in the trust and esteem of his hearers, and gained as the wage of character or service."[1]

This last admonition cannot be too strongly emphasized. Let no man speak on these themes

[1] Rev. J. Brierley, in London *Christian World*, July 25, 1901.

who has not qualified himself by careful study; who does not thoroughly know what he is talking about. There is a great deal of crude preaching on social questions, the whole effect of which is mischievous. I have known men to prepare themselves, by two or three months' study, to give courses of lectures on these themes before theological seminaries. Every week I am receiving letters from ministers, who say that they have given no attention to such subjects, and who wish me to put them in possession of material for sermons or addresses to be delivered within a week or two. The breadth and complexity of these social questions are but dimly apprehended by many who dabble in them. This is no reason for avoiding them; but it is a reason for making diligent preparation to speak upon them. Many of the subjects on which we must speak call for patient and thorough study; to evade them because of their difficulty would be infidelity to our trust; we must earnestly seek to master them.

With the work of the leading modern economists and sociologists every minister ought to be acquainted. Not that he is to preach economics or sociology; but he needs to be familiar with the constructive ideas on which these sciences are based, and with the facts by which they are supported. In the work of some of

these students of society he will find much that
will greatly aid him, for there are not a few of
them to whom the larger aspects of these problems are fully revealed. But the Christian
student must always be on his guard against a
pseudo-science which ignores the spiritual realm,
and bases social laws upon an induction in which
the larger half of human nature is neglected.
A good deal of economic theory rests upon a
purely materialistic foundation; upon assump-
tions which deny human freedom, and the play
of the moral forces; upon the notion that the
laws of human nature are of the same order as
those of gravitation and chemical affinity. The
fact for you and me to keep steadily before us
is that human society is under the sway of spiritual motives; that it is constantly undergoing
renovation through the ideals which men entertain and the choices which they make; that human nature is modifiable, and is constantly being modified, under the influence of the divine
Spirit, so that social standards and ruling ideas
are gradually changing from generation to generation. This is not mere sentiment; it is the
scientific fact, the historic fact, just as verifiable
as any law of chemistry or biology, and we are
to take our stand upon it, and insist upon inter-
preting the phenomena of society in the light of
the spiritual laws. With the politics and the

economics which are separated from the spiritual realm and which rest, whether avowedly or implicitly, upon a materialistic basis, we have nothing to do, except to show their defectiveness. But if we need to study the heresies of past and present ages in order that we may be able, under the cross-lights of this investigation, more clearly to apprehend the truth of Christianity, there is certainly no less need that we should be familiar with defective theories of social relations, in order that we may the better understand the true theory which supplements and corrects them. And as in the study of the heresies we always find some truth which we need to know, so in our study even of materialistic economics we shall discover many facts of deep significance.

The truth which Mr. Brierley emphasizes in the passage which I last read is the truth which we must never forget. The church, he says, will have these social subjects "continually within its scope, but ever to bring them under its own light, to view them *sub specie æternitatis*." Yea, verily. We have absolutely no business whatever with any of these things except as they are vitally and inseparably related to that kingdom of heaven for whose coming we pray, whose presence we ought to be quick to discern, and whose spread it is our first business to seek. "When the minister has become merely political," says Mr. Brierley, "it is because he has lost grip of religion." That proposition ought to require no argument. The minister who has become merely or mainly political, or sociological, or economical, or scientific, has abandoned his vocation. The minister to whom religion is not the central and culminating power in all his teaching has no right in any Christian pulpit. It is *the religion* of politics, of economics, of sociology that we are to teach, — nothing else. We are to bring the truths and the powers of the spiritual world, the eternal world, to bear upon all these themes. This is what we have to do with these social questions, and we have nothing else to do with them.

The first thing for us to understand is that God is in his world, and that we are workers together with him. In all this industrial struggle he is present in every part of it, working according to the counsel of his perfect will. In the gleams of light which sometimes break forth from the darkness of the conflict we discern his inspiration; in the stirrings of goodwill which temper the wasting strife we behold the evidence of his presence; in the sufferings and losses and degradations which wait upon every violation of his law of love we witness the retributions with which that law goes armed. In the weltering masses of poverty; in the giddy throngs that tread the paths of vice; in the multitudes distressed and scattered as sheep having no shepherd; in the brutalized ranks marching in lock-step through the prison yard; in the groups of politicians scheming for place and plunder, — in all the most forlorn and untoward and degrading human associations, the One who is never absent is that divine Spirit which brooded over the chaos at the beginning, nursing it to life and beauty, and which is

> " nearer to every creature it hath made,
> Than anything unto itself."

Nay, there is not one of these hapless, sinning multitudes in whose spirit he is not present to will and to work according to his good pleasure; never overpowering their will, but gently pressing in, by every avenue open to him, his gifts of love and truth. As he has for every man's life a plan, so has he for the common life a perfect social order into which he seeks to lead his children, that he may give them plenty and blessedness and abundance of peace as long as the moon endureth. Surely he has a way for men to live in society; he has a way of organizing industry; he has a way of life for the family, and for the school, and for the shop, and for the city, and for the state; he has a way for preventing poverty, and a way for helping and saving the poor and the sick and the sinful; and it is his way that we are to seek and point out and follow. We cannot know it perfectly, but if we are humble and faithful and obedient, we shall come to understand it better and better as the years go by. The one thing for us to be sure of is that God has a way for human beings to live and work together, just as truly as he has a way for the stars over our heads and the crystals under our feet; and that it is man's chief end to find this way and follow it.

"What the world really wants," says the teacher I have quoted, "is men who have news from the land of the ideal, who have God's life within them, who open afresh the springs of living water that quench the thirst of the soul." Nothing can be truer. But for what kind of news from the land of the ideal are men hungering and thirsting? For the news that brings the ideal down to earth; that makes it no mere dreamy possibility of far-off good, but the lamp of our feet and the light of our path now and here. For all this common life of ours there are ideals that uplift and transfigure and ennoble it. There is an ideal for the home and for the church, for the school and for the shop, for the factory and for the city; and the one refreshing and inspiring experience of life is to get sight of it, and believe in it. The ideal in all these social organizations is nothing else but God's way, — the way that he has ordained for human beings to live and work together. The thing for us to do is first to discern it ourselves, and then to get men to see it, and believe in it, and work for it with heart and soul and mind and strength. It will not be realized all at once; it will take long years of labor and patience; but it is the

> "far-off divine event
> To which the whole creation moves,"

and we know that there can be no permanent peace or welfare but that to which it beckons us.

I trust, my brethren, that I have made plain to you my own deep conviction that the work of the ministry in these days must be deeply concerned with social questions. I trust that you will all find in your own hearts a growing interest in these questions, and that you will be able to communicate that interest to the people to whom you are sent; to kindle in their hearts the enthusiasm of humanity, and to guide them in their thoughts and labors for their fellow men. And I trust that you can also see that this social teaching and social service is not something outside of religion; that religion is and must be the heart and soul of it all; that it means nothing but religion coming to reality in everyday life; the divine ideal descending upon human society and transforming it from glory to glory, even as by the spirit of the Lord. If there is any treatment of social questions in the pulpit which has any other aim or inspiration than this, I have no faith in it. If any minister thinks that he can wisely separate these questions from religion and treat them upon the basis of economic theory or political expediency, I do not agree with him. I do not, for my own part, expect to see any radical or permanent cure discovered for poverty or pauperism, for grinding monopoly or municipal corruption, for bribery or debauchery or crime, except as men's minds and hearts are opened to receive the truths of the spiritual world; except as they are brought into conscious and vital relations with things unseen and eternal. There can be no adequate social reform save that which springs from a genuine revival of religion; only it must be a religion which is less concerned about getting men to heaven than about fitting them for their proper work on the earth; which does not set itself over against the secular life in contrast, but enters into the secular life and subdues it by its power and rules it by its law, and transfigures it by its light. For any other kind of religion than this I do not think that the world has any longer very much use.

May God fill your lives with it, and teach you how to bring home its truth and reality to the hearts of men.

II

THE CARE OF THE POOR

THE social question which is likely first to present itself to the mind of the conscientious pastor is the condition and needs of the poor who live within the territory for whose care as pastor he feels himself responsible. It may be that he will find a small number of poor families connected with his congregation, but there is reason to fear that the number of really needy families will be very small indeed in almost any congregation to which you are likely to be called. If when Jesus said, "The poor ye have always with you," he meant, "in your churches," his prediction is not, in our day, generally fulfilled. The reason of this is, in part, that the greater number of the really needy have become so by reason of defective moral conduct which, according to our Congregational theory of church-membership, would exclude them from the fellowship of the church. Yet there is also, I fear, a serious failure on the part of most of our churches to comprehend the full meaning of the Parable of the Lost Sheep, and to put forth the kind of effort in seeking and saving the lost which Jesus expects of his disciples.

So far as the poor have been drawn into the fellowship of the church and surrounded by its saving influences, the care of them has ceased to be a social question. Respecting your relation to them you have been instructed in your lectures on pastoral theology. It is the poor who are outside all churches, or but slenderly connected with them, of whom we are thinking now. We have them always near us, if not with us; and the relation of the minister and the church to this multitude distressed and scattered, as sheep not having a shepherd, presents a serious problem to every young minister.

When I speak of the poor I mean those who are living, much of the time, in destitution and penury; who are frequently out of work, and suffering for lack of the necessaries of life; who are apt to apply to charitable agencies, or to the officers of the city or the town, for assistance. That the proportion of this class to the entire population has been rapidly increasing since the civil war, there can be no doubt. Statistics on the subject are unsatisfactory, owing to the lack of uniformity in the methods by which they are compiled; but my own pretty careful observation, in a ministry covering this entire period, convinces me that such is the case.

The reasons for this increase are not far to seek.

The rapid shifting of industries, by which many laborers are displaced, and the frequent periods of industrial depression have thrown many temporarily out of employment; in such enforced leisure, habits of idleness and dependence are formed which tend to become chronic.

The multiplication of machinery, the concentration of business, and the stress of competition are driving the entire industrial mechanism at a greatly accelerated speed, and only the most efficient and adaptable are wanted; laborers of low intelligence and little skill find it increasingly difficult to keep in the movement; they are flung off, in large numbers, and left to the care of charity.

The growth of wealth in the hands of those who are more compassionate than judicious also tends to propagate dependence and poverty; the presence in any community of a considerable fund of money, and superfluous food, and partly worn clothing, ready to be distributed, without careful investigation, by impulsive and sentimental givers, constitutes an effective demand for mendicancy, and the supply is unfailing.

The increasing number of charitable funds and institutions has the same effect. The knowledge that those in any given community who can make out a fairly good case of destitution will receive aid draws to that community the shiftless and improvident from the country round about. In the city where I live I can name quite a number of families that have been added to our population within the last twenty years for this reason. In their country homes they were well known, and their claims upon compassion would have been more sharply questioned ; the city offered a much more promising opportunity to those who were willing to be dependent.

We may add to these causes the loose administration of public outdoor relief in most of our cities. That the public funds for the relief of the poor in their homes are distributed generally upon wholly inadequate investigation, and sometimes with corrupt intent, — to reward party services or to gain votes, — is not to be doubted.

What may be called the natural causes of poverty are always at work — sickness, accident, inherited infirmity, or disability; but we have been considering the reasons for the *proportional* increase in the number of dependents; and we find these reasons, partly in unwonted economic disturbances, partly in injudicious charity, and partly in bad political administration. Some of these causes are at least in part removable, as we shall see in subsequent discussions.

But whatever the causes may be, the conditions confront us everywhere. The statisticians tell us that our wealth per capita has been mounting up, decade by decade, with almost incredible rapidity, but the number of dependents gains upon the population. In every considerable community there are those who derive part if not all of their subsistence from public or private charity. Even the smaller cities have their slums, where the conditions of life are most depressing, and groups of the miserable are within the sound of most of our church bells. With these, it is evident, we have some important business. However they came to be where they are, they are there, within our reach, and they need our help. It matters not at all whether they are worthy or unworthy — unless it be that the unworthy have the stronger claim; it was the unworthy, rather than the worthy, that Christ came to call.

The care of these destitute and dependent persons has been generally relegated by the churches to the public authorities or the charity organizations. In treatises on pastoral theology, the responsibility of the church for work of this kind has commonly been disclaimed or ignored. It is doubtless true, as we shall see, that a large part of this work may be done through the coöperation of the church either with other churches or with charitable societies. But much may be done by the local church, on its own impulse, and without waiting for any. Indeed, I am inclined to believe that if the local churches were alive to their opportunity, the greater part of this work would be done by them, in the best possible way.

The thing for the church to aim at is to put itself into relations of personal friendship with as many families of this dependent class as it can reach and care for. The aim of the Boston Associated Charities, as its distinguished president has told us in a memorable phrase, is to provide for every poor family a friend. The whole meaning and value of the true charity is in that phrase. And what the Associated Charities thus proposes should be the definite aim of every Christian church — to provide for every poor family that it can reach one wise, faithful, sympathetic friend.

The acquaintance of these families is best made through some Sunday-school, or sewing-school, into which the children are first gathered. If the church is happily situated, as mine is, in the heart of the city and in the midst of a population needing ministry of this kind, then the church can call into its own buildings the children of these poor families, and make its own consecrated temple a point of attraction for them. If the church is not thus fortunately located, it may be necessary for it to find quarters for work of this kind in closer proximity to the needy field.

The children, thus gathered, are to be considered not mainly as subjects of Biblical or industrial instruction, though that is not to be neglected, but mainly as human beings in need of friendship, to whom, and to whose households, this device has opened the door. Some of their mothers will come with them, and now and then a father will appear, leading his child by the hand. By this means the church will be able to put itself into direct relations with a certain number of families of the very poor. For this service it will need a volunteer band of friendly visitors, the most cultivated, the most wise, the most consecrated men and women in its membership. The Sunday-school teachers cannot begin to do this work; for each Sunday-school teacher or sewing-school teacher may have half a dozen or a dozen families represented in her class, and the best results are gained in this friendly visiting when no visitor has more than one family to care for. This makes the matter more individual; the visitor cannot have the feeling that she is doing wholesale work, — that she is dealing with a class; she is simply the friend of this family; the relation between herself and them is more apt to become what it ought to be, a strictly personal relation. I am using the feminine pronouns, because they are likely to be more frequently applicable; but this work ought not to be confined to women; in many cases men can do it quite as efficiently, and for their own sakes the men of the churches ought to have a large part in it.

The purpose of this visitation should be kept as far as possible from the lines of ordinary almsgiving. Cases will arise in which material aid must be given, but this is not the main object, and should be kept wholly in the background. Indeed, it will be better if the visitor contrive to have such aid, when it is needed, reach the family through other hands than his own. He wants to be a friend, more than an almoner. If the cause of the poverty is lack of employment, or incapacity, or discouragement, or what we might call moral prostration, — which is, I fear, a prevalent malady, — their deepest need is spiritual, not material; they want friendship even more than food and coal; they must be helped to get on their feet and support themselves; work must be found for them; their hope and self-respect must be stimulated; the door of opportunity must be opened and held open before them.

This work of the friendly visitor is the heart and life of all the most intelligent charity of this day. The organized charities have learned to emphasize it and rely upon it; the best forms of state aid, as, for example, those which prevail in the German cities, make it fundamental. The one thing needful in all these efforts to rescue and elevate the dependent classes is the touch of life upon life, the awakening of hope and courage, the invigoration of character. The high calling of the charity-worker is nothing less than the salvation of souls — that is, of men and women and children — for these are the only souls we know. To save a soul from ruin is simply to save a man or woman from ruin; and the character is the thing to be saved. The mere relief of physical suffering or want which does not have the effect to restore and strengthen the manhood and womanhood is a superficial and temporary service. "It may appear," says Mr. Alfred T. White of Brooklyn, a wise and devoted laborer in this great field, "a slow process to eliminate poverty piece by piece from our great cities, and it is natural to long for some quicker way; but there is no way which does not reach to and touch the character of the individual poor."[1]

If such is the essential character of the best

[1] *Charities Review*, April, 1893.

work for the dependent classes, then the field is certainly wide open to the local church in every community. The less machinery and organization there is connected with it, the better. It is a work which calls for no constitution and by-laws, no minutes, no public meetings, no reports. You must find some discreet, large-hearted man or woman who will take charge of it, keeping a list of the families who need friends, and finding for each the friend who appears to be best adapted to this particular case. That is all there is to do. Friendship is not a matter of rules and regulations; this ambassador of good-will must be permitted to find his own way into the confidence of the household thus committed to him, and must develop his friendship along individual lines. It might be well to put into the hands of each of these visitors some brief statement of the nature of the work like that published by the Brooklyn Bureau of Charities: —

"It shall be the duty of a friendly visitor to visit the poor and distressed as a friend; to examine, in the spirit of kindness, the causes of their trouble; to do what can be done to remove those causes; to become acquainted with the ability which each may have, and to aid in developing it and in finding ways in which it may be employed in self-help; through friendly intercourse, sympathy, and direction to encourage self-dependence, industry, and thrift; to recommend whatever may be possible and wise to alleviate the sufferings of those whose infirmities cannot be cured or removed; if material aid be necessary, to obtain it from existing organizations as far as possible; and in every case to promote in all practical ways the physical and moral improvement of the families in the visitor's charge."

The member of the church who is superintending this work should watch to see that the visitors are keeping in contact with the families intrusted to them; and there may be occasional private consultations and conferences among the visitors respecting the problems which arise; but there should be no public statements concerning their work; your friend does not go into a public meeting and recite what he knows about your personal and family affairs.

It is not necessary to say that work of this kind will not all be well done. No kind of work that we attempt is uniformly well done. There is a great deal of bungling and blundering and shirking in our best organizations. There is a great deal of poor preaching, and poor pastoral administration, and poor Sunday-school teaching, and poor financial management; the defects and failures of our best endeavors are always in sight. This kind of work requires greater wisdom, truer insight, finer character, than almost anything else that we attempt, and it goes without saying that there will be many cases in which it will prove a failure or a very indifferent success. Some of these visitors will lack the sympathy, the tact, the courage needful for their delicate business, and they will sooner or later abandon it, with pessimistic conclusions as to the possibility of doing any good to the poor. But there will be others who will persevere and succeed; who will learn how, without violating the personality of those to whom they go, to establish confidential and helpful relations with them, and the gains of these friendships will not all be on the side of the visited.

With families which are in this relation to the church much can be done to enlarge and brighten life. I know one church in which there are thirty or forty friendly visitors, each with her single family; and once a month the visitors and the mothers of these families meet in the parlors of the church for a social afternoon, drinking a cup of tea together and listening to a familiar talk from some woman physician on health, or on the care of children, or on the preparation of food for the sick; or enjoying the recital of some one's experiences of travel.

or the reading of a story or a poem. Every other week, through the winter season, the same church offers in its chapel a free popular entertainment consisting of elementary lectures on science, with experiments; or a lantern exhibition; or a practical talk about life, — all enlivened by the best music. These entertainments are crowded by the older children of the Sunday-school and the sewing-school, with a goodly number of their parents and older brothers and sisters and neighbors.

Thus does the church reach out, with humanizing and helpful influences, into the lives of those who are most in need of the grace that bringeth salvation. And I can think of no reason why work of this kind should not be undertaken, immediately, by every Christian church. Certainly it is the kind of work that our Lord would be doing if he were here; and any group of disciples who are in close sympathy with him will find in their hearts an immediate and irresistible desire to engage in service of this kind.

Doubtless many churches shrink from the thought of ministering to the poor because they are financially weak; it is difficult for them to meet their current expenses, and they think that they have no funds which could be used in such ministration. But it should be remembered that the kind of work here proposed does not involve any large expenditure. There are exceptional cases in which the visitor will need a little money or some form of material aid, but that can be obtained. If the visitor herself is not able to furnish it, she can find some one in the neighborhood who is both able and willing. There are few American communities in which supplies may not be promptly and easily found for any well-attested cases of need. There are multitudes of men and women who are more than willing to give, if they can be assured that their gifts will relieve suffering. The visitor who can bring any case of real destitution to the notice of some benevolent individual is in that way rendering a real service to him that gives as well as to him that receives. The church does not, then, need to provide any considerable fund for the relief of the poor, when it enters upon work of this kind. The existence of such a fund would be an embarrassment rather than an aid to its work. It is friendship, not alms, that it is undertaking to dispense; and no church is so poor that it cannot offer friendship to some of the friendless who live within its reach. In truth, the most efficient aid which is given to the poor comes from those who themselves are poor. The sympathy and helpfulness which are always found among these lowly neighbors are beautiful to see.

The fact that the revenues of a church are not large is not, then, a good reason why it should hesitate to commission and send forth a group of friendly visitors. It may be well to remember that the first company which went forth on an errand of this nature consisted wholly of poor men, and that He who sent them forth was no richer than they.

If all our Christian churches should accept this as part of their mission — to put themselves in communication with as many needy families, outside their own membership, as they could find and wisely care for, I think that the problem of relief for the outside poor — for those who should be cared for in their homes, rather than in institutions — would be promptly solved. There are few American communities in which the churches are not numerous enough and strong enough to do this work without any serious effort.

In the country at large there is about one church to every four hundred and twenty-five of the population. Except in the great industrial depressions, it would be hard to find an American community in which six per cent. of the population were dependent. If the average church is responsible for four hundred and twenty-five of the population, six per cent. of that number would be about twenty-five persons, or, perhaps, five families. The average church could undertake that amount of care, with no strain upon its resources. Nay, such an undertaking, in most cases, would replenish and invigorate its life, in every way; would mightily strengthen its hold upon the community; would give it a reason for its life which now it often lacks.

If, however, the churches generally should take up work of this kind, it would at once be necessary for them to come to some understanding with one another about it. They would soon be crossing one another's tracks and duplicating one another's work. It would be needful that they should divide up the field among them, assigning to each church a definite district, in which it should be responsible for the care of its own poor, and of all poor families not belonging to other congregations.

This seems to me the ideal way of taking care of the poor. I believe that the churches could do the work; that it would not greatly tax their resources, if they did it in the right way; that it would deepen and strengthen their Christian life; that it would do more to shut the mouths of cavilers than all the arguments of all the apologists; that it would help to solve the question of reaching the churchless; that it would marvelously extend the influence and the usefulness of the churches.

I trust, therefore, my brethren, that you will keep this before you, in all your ministry, as the ideal method of caring for those of the poor who can be best assisted in their own homes. It may be a good while before we shall get the churches generally to accept this responsibility and to coöperate in bearing it; but I believe that the time will come, and it may be nearer than we think. The deplorable inefficiency of most of the existing methods of public outdoor relief; the too obvious fact that by what we miscall charity multitudes are pauperized; the fearful losses of character and manhood that we are suffering in this way, must at length bring home to the churches their duty in this matter. And the churches may be able to see that they need the work quite as much as the work needs them; that they can only save their own life by losing it in such ministry as this.

In some of our cities serious attempts have been made to work along this line. The most persistent and successful of these of which I have known is in Buffalo. The churches there have undertaken to divide the entire city among themselves, and to assign to each church a district, for the poor families of which it shall hold itself responsible.[1] Some smaller communities have adopted substantially the same plan. Pos-

[1] *The Christian Pastor*, p. 467, *seq.*

sibly the movements toward church federation which are now going forward, in various parts of the country, with considerable promise, may come to include this practical endeavor. I hope that many of you will live long enough to take part in a successful prosecution of some such enterprise.

But you may find it wise to content yourselves at the outset with methods which come short of this ideal. In the communities where you are called to labor, it may not be possible at once to revolutionize the methods of poor relief. You are likely to find in the larger places a variety of agencies already at work in this field. Societies for the collection and distribution of charitable relief exist in most of our cities; and there are soldiers' aid societies and beneficial organizations of various names, as well as churches, engaged in the same enterprise. Coöperation of all these agencies is greatly to be desired. It is of the greatest importance that all the charitable organizations at work in a given community should not only have a good understanding among themselves, but that each should have some knowledge of what the others are doing, and that all should unite upon certain principles of administration. If they work independently, the shiftless and unscrupulous will make themselves the beneficiaries of several of them at once, and they will breed **imposture** and pauperism. It is absolutely necessary that the charitable forces be united to prevent the propagation of pauperism.

In many places you will find the charities thus organized, and you ought to give that enterprise your hearty and intelligent support. These charity organization societies do not receive, in any community, the support they deserve; in the minds of many sentimental people there is much prejudice against them. They are sometimes sneeringly called "societies for the prevention of charity," and it is, indeed, an important part of their work to prevent a great deal of miscalled charity. The amount of injury which is done by careless almsgiving is appalling. The great majority of our Christian people look no further than the immediate relief of what seems to them suffering or need; their sensibilities are touched by a child in rags or a tale of woe; a gift of money or food or fuel alleviates their own personal discomfort and makes them feel virtuous, and thus by a dole they relieve themselves without thinking or caring much of what becomes of the receiver. The fact that they may be encouraging a man to become a beggar, or leading a child into the ways of ruin, does not greatly trouble them. What we call our charity is often the expression of one of the subtlest and most mischievous forms of selfishness.

You are likely to find, in the churches to which you will go, a good many people who need to be educated out of these sentimental notions about charity, and to be made to understand the principles upon which the work of charity organizations is carried on. These principles are, as I believe, for the most part, not only sound and expedient, they are thoroughly Christian. There may have been, in the earlier days, a little too much emphasis on the prevention of imposture and pauperism, but that disproportion, if it ever existed, has disappeared; whatever severities are practiced in these methods of administration are the severities of a genuine love. The reason why modern charity-workers are so careful about the bestowment of material aid is that they value so highly the real welfare of those with whom they are dealing. They know that suffering is a far less evil than moral deterioration; they would choose for themselves hunger or cold rather than the spirit of a mendicant; and it is because they love their neighbors as themselves that they make the same choice for them.

This principle does not relieve the charity-worker of responsibility or labor; it adds to his load and doubles his task. It is an easy thing to telephone your grocer to send a little flour and rice and ham and sugar and tea to the street number from which some suppliant for aid has come to your door; it is a very different thing to go over there, and get acquainted with that family, and find out all about their condition and their needs, and the causes of their present destitution, to find work for those who can work, to awaken and strengthen the purpose of self-help, and having got them on their feet, to stand by them and cheer them on, and stimulate in every way their courage and independence. To such painstaking service as this the modern charity-worker is pledged, and it takes time and thought and love and long-suffering patience. He does not cavil at the command of Jesus, "Give to him that asketh thee, and from him that would borrow of thee, turn not thou away;" he accepts the word, without reserve, and means to obey it. But he does not understand that command to mean that we must give, in all cases, the specific thing asked for. If a man asks for poison, or for a murderous weapon, or for a pure young life that he may pollute it, we are not to give the thing he craves. If he asks for money, and we are morally certain that he will use the money to degrade himself, we are not warranted by the command of Jesus in giving him the money. But if a man asks us to help him, and we can see that he needs anything that we are able to give him, we are pledged to supply that need. His appeal to us warrants our interposition in his behalf. He has confessed that he needs our friendship, and we have a right to take him at his word. Our friendship he shall have, and we will do our best to make it a wise and saving friendship. The things that he really needs are the things that we will try to provide for him; they may not be the things which he craves; but it is to needs, not to cravings, that we are called to minister.

These are the principles on which the modern charity is building. They are, as I have said, distinctively Christian principles. They involve what is central in Christianity — a supreme valuation of character; a recognition of the fact that physical suffering is a far less evil than moral degradation. There are a good many hundreds of thousands of people in all our churches who have, as yet, very feebly comprehended these principles. There is need of much education by the pulpit along this line. The genuinely Christian work of the charity organization visitors is often greatly crippled by the heedless almsgiving of lazy church members who feed tramps and give doles to beggars. An important part of your work will be to get a little more intelligence into the heads and a little more conscience into the hearts of these sentimentalists; to show them what the Christian law requires them to do to the neighbor who appeals to them for aid; and to bring them into a hearty coöperation with those who are working not merely to relieve immediate want, but to save men and women.

Those members of your congregation who are themselves engaged in the work of the friendly visitor will, of course, be instructed in these things; but it is highly important that the whole congregation be brought into sympathy and co-operation with efforts which are made for the systematic and intelligent administration of the charities of the entire community. The friendly visitor of the church is doing exactly the same kind of work that the charity organization society is doing. The friendly visitor is the right arm of the charity organization society. Some of the members of your churches may be working under that society, and the methods of both should be essentially the same.

Let me repeat, that the ideal organization of charity would be a compact union of all the Christian churches in every community, covering the entire field and making all other agencies for the care of the outside poor unnecessary. Until this is accomplished, charity organization societies are necessary to unite and direct the various agencies occupying the field. With these organizations you should bring your church into hearty sympathy and coöperation; lending your members for its service, since it supplements the work which your church is doing. Your church should, however, at the same time, keep itself in vital touch with the poor families of its neighborhood by its own corps of friendly visitors.

I have alluded to the fact that the needs of the poor are in part supplied by public relief, dispensed by the town or the city or the county. This is of two kinds — indoor and outdoor relief.

Those who are permanently disabled and helpless, and who have no friends to whose care they may rightfully be committed, must be provided with homes in the almshouses and infirmaries. The children of broken families, in some of our states, are cared for in children's homes until other homes can be found for them, and this is a most wise and benign provision, for children should never be mixed with the adult paupers of an almshouse. For these institutions the state must needs provide; but the Christian people of every community ought to keep vigilant watch over them, to see that they are well governed. Indoor relief is the business of the state; the relation of the pulpit and the church to that is simply that of careful supervision, to see that the business is well done.

With those who are in temporary straits because of sickness or misfortune, and who should be cared for in their own homes, the case is somewhat different. It is generally admitted in Christian countries that the state is under obligation to provide for such need; the laws recognize this obligation; part of the money raised by taxation is devoted to the relief of those temporarily in distress. The motive is humane. The incorporation in our law of the principle of brotherly kindness is a sign of the progress of the kingdom. But, in practice, this method of public outdoor relief has not been working very well in this country. In the smaller communities its failure is less notable; in the larger towns and cities the abuses connected with it outweigh its benefits. The investigation of cases applying for aid is wholly inadequate; the idle and the thriftless and the vicious learn to depend upon it and are degraded by it; it is used, not seldom, by unscrupulous officials, as a means of controlling votes. The evils arising from the distribution of legal outdoor relief are often very grave.

In Germany this does not appear to be the case. In all the German cities the work is thoroughly systematized; the cities are divided into

THE CARE OF THE POOR 57

small districts, in each of which several of the most respectable and responsible men and women are appointed and required to serve as visitors, so that the work of investigation and relief is done under the supervision of the public authorities with great care and thoroughness. In Berlin, for example, something like three thousand of the best citizens are employed as visitors of the poor. They receive no remuneration, but they are not permitted to decline such service; they accept it as one of their public obligations. If we could hope to get this kind of work done gratuitously and faithfully by Americans, the legal outdoor relief of the poor would be a simple problem. But that, I fear, would be a visionary expectation. In my own city of 125,000 people, one man, who gives part of his time to the business, and receives a salary of $60 a month, is expected to do the entire work of investigation — the cases on which he must decide including two or three thousand families every year. It is evident that funds administered in this way will be worse than wasted.

What is to be desired is either that the city should abandon the work of outdoor relief, leaving it to the voluntary agencies, or else that it should enter into a close coöperation with these voluntary agencies, employing them to do the work of investigation, and administering its relief on their recommendation.

In quite a number of our most important American cities, — New York, Philadelphia, and Baltimore among them, — the work of legal outdoor relief has been wholly abandoned. It may be supposed that this would have the effect to increase the number seeking refuge in the almshouses. The contrary seems to be the case. When Brooklyn, several years ago, cut off legal outdoor relief, the number of persons in the almshouses decreased, instead of increasing. The outdoor relief, as administered, was encouraging pauperism, was breeding paupers, in fact; when the city stopped that bad business, one of the sources from which her almshouses were supplied with their permanent population was dried up. The people who were learning to depend on charity were compelled to look out for themselves, and the habit of self-help to which they were coerced kept them out of the poorhouse.

It is, however, difficult to bring many of our cities to the point of cutting off outdoor relief, and it is not always the case that the voluntary charities are so well organized that they could efficiently care for all the poor who need relief in their homes. But it is possible, in many cases, to bring about a coöperation between the charity organization society and the town or city authorities, so that the city shall make use

THE CARE OF THE POOR 59

of the voluntary agency in making its investigations, and shall thus be enabled to do its work more intelligently and with less injury to the community. In Ohio the law now permits the officers having the distribution of the poor funds to employ the officers of the charity organization societies as their agents, and to govern themselves in dispensing aid by the advice so given. This was done, whether with or without legal authorization I do not know, in the city of Springfield, Massachusetts, when I was living there; and the result was not only a great reduction in the cost of outdoor relief to the city, but a manifest decrease in the amount of poverty and beggary. No really needy cases were neglected, and a great multitude of idlers and shirkers were compelled to go to work. When the charity organization is efficient and the overseers of the poor are reasonable, such a coöperation can be brought about with great gains of economy, of thrift, and of morality. It is one of the subjects concerning which every Christian minister, as a leader of public opinion, ought to keep himself well informed, and one of the ends which, wherever it is practicable, he should endeavor to secure.

In considering the relief of the poor in their homes, therefore, the thing to be aimed at is the transfer of this work as rapidly as possible, and to as great an extent as is possible, from the public authorities to voluntary agencies — either to churches or to organized charities. The reason is that the public authorities in this country, even when their intentions are good, are so few that they cannot adequately perform the work, and that it is a kind of work which cannot be well performed by state officials. It is a work, the very heart of which, as we have seen, is friendship. It can be well done only by those who have a deep and strong sense of spiritual values, of the supreme importance of character. It is essentially a work of redemption, and it calls for love and service and sacrifice. May God help us all to see how much there is for us to do in our ministry, in filling up that which is lacking of the afflictions of Christ, and in seeking and saving the lost.

III

THE STATE AND THE UNEMPLOYED

We have considered the importance of extending and strengthening the voluntary agencies for the relief of the poor, and of transferring to these agencies, so far as possible, the work now done for the outside poor by the state. There remains, however, a work for the state to do, outside its almshouses and its children's homes, in dealing with the problem of poverty. There is a certain important work to be done which no voluntary organization can succeed in doing, — a work which requires the exercise of the power of the state.

We have, to begin with, periods of depression more or less regularly occurring, in which a large proportion of the population is out of work. These industrial crises are sometimes supposed to be mysterious visitations of Providence, and they are sometimes charged upon the political party which happens to be in power, but I do not think that either Providence or the politicians should bear the blame.

The explanation is probably very simple. So long as the credit system exists and human nature is what it now is, everybody will borrow of everybody else, and live on what he borrows. Thus credit is more and more extended, until some of the more cautious begin to take alarm, and to demand payment. The retail merchants send out bills to their customers and press for payment, and the customers, because they cannot pay, stop buying. The merchants must therefore stop ordering from the jobbers, and the jobbers from the manufacturers, and the mill wheels stop and the men are out of work, and the great commercial wheel ceases its revolutions. It is not started again until a great many of the debts owed by everybody to everybody are canceled, and there is a tremendous shrinkage in the nominal wealth of the nation.

Whatever may be the causes of these depressions, they return, periodically, and while they last there is much suffering. In such emergencies it is generally felt that private charity is inadequate, and that the state must come to the rescue. I am not inclined to dispute this contention, yet even in such times I believe that the good-will of good men and women, if it were roused to action, could greatly reduce the need of public intervention. It is far better that relief come through individual initiative; a loan, at low rates of interest, proffered to an industrious man by one who knows him well and can trust him, would often be a wise beneficence. But better than this is the provision of work which can often be made by individuals who have a surplus which they might employ as wages. There are always, in such times, individuals who have a little money and much goodwill, and who feel called upon to give liberally to the relief funds to be administered by certain charities. It would be better if they would begin some enterprise of repair or improvement upon their houses or their grounds and would set idle men at work upon it, paying out as wages what they intend to give in charity. If the work is not greatly needed, it will be a far greater benefaction to furnish it than to bestow alms upon idle laborers. In view of the fact that the work is not needed, the wages offered may fairly be less than those paid in flush times, and the trade-unions, in such cases, should relax their demands. Thus there is an economic adjustment, and the man of good-will serves himself as well as his neighbor by getting his work done more cheaply in the hard times. I am persuaded that if the attention of kind-hearted people were called to this matter, and the efficiency and beneficence of this kind of relief were brought home to them, a great many private relief agencies of this sort would be set in operation, the effect of which would be far better than that of the ordinary methods of emergency relief.

It is a matter concerning which you may sometimes be warranted in speaking from the pulpit. One preaches a great many sermons concerning which he never knows whether any one heeds them or not; but now and then one hears from a sermon, afterward, not merely that somebody liked it, but that it set somebody to work. One or two of the sermons from which I have thus heard were preached in the midst of such seasons of depression, setting forth the value of the kind of help for the unemployed of which I have been speaking. As the result of one such sermon, one man, I remember, set about building two or three houses on unoccupied lots; several others made repairs or improvements, of one sort or another, on their premises; one man started a little business of buying up apples and potatoes in the country and bringing them to the city by car-loads, in which he gave employment to three or four persons; and quite a number of others, who had intended to discharge various employees, thought better of it and determined to keep them and pay them wages instead of contributing to the relief fund the amount which they might have saved in the reduction of their expenditure. If all Christian people were as thoughtful and considerate and mindful of their opportunities as they ought to be in such times, the need of public provision for the unemployed would be greatly minimized, and many families would be kept from entering upon the slippery ways of dependency.

But, as things are, it is often true that the city or the town must intervene for the relief of industrious people whose means of livelihood has failed them. There are emergencies when the resources of private charity are inadequate, and when there will be much suffering unless the public authorities provide some measures of aid for the unemployed. The difficulty in such cases is that many come forward to claim the aid thus provided who are not honestly entitled to it, and to whom it is an injury rather than a benefit. This, indeed, is the difficulty which constantly presents itself in the administration of charity, both public and private. In every army of the unemployed there is a certain number of the unemployable, — of men and women who are never employed, if they can help themselves, in good times, and to whom hard times are a godsend because their excuse for idleness cannot then be questioned.

I do not know whether you are now taught,

in this seminary, to make a distinction between natural inability and moral inability; that distinction was once familiar, and it is one for which the charity-worker has frequent use. There is a considerable class of the very poor in all our towns and cities whose inability to work is strictly moral. It is this class of persons which presents the standing problem in all our efforts to help the poor. The man who does not want to work, who prefers to eat his bread in the sweat of some other man's (or woman's) brow, is not unknown to the student of sociology.

The existence of this class is, however, sometimes questioned. There are philanthropists and social reformers who maintain that the people who are out of work are willing to work; that their lack of employment is the fault of society; that under a proper social system this class would disappear or cause no trouble. Those who hold this view are, however, persons who have never come into any close and continuous practical relations with this class of the population. Any one who has been dealing for thirty or forty years with the unemployed has learned some things about them which the social theorists have never found out, but which it is highly important for them to know before they launch their millenniums.

By reflection upon the social phenomena with which we are all familiar, we might easily assure ourselves that many of the people in the lowest social class would avoid work if they could. Is not that the truth concerning many people in the upper social classes? Is there not in all circles a pretty large number of those who will get their living if they can without exertion, — who will shift their burdens, when they can, upon other people's shoulders? Those of keen wits and large opportunities manage to do this and get their living out of society, sometimes to fare sumptuously every day; those of dull wits and narrow opportunities do not succeed so well, and their last resource is the soup-kitchen and the free lodging-house. But it would be flying in the face of all experience to insist that all these workless people are willing and eager to work — that they lack only opportunity; if that were true of them, they would be unlike every other class in society.

I am sure that many of those who are out of work would rather work than beg or be dependent, just as there are many self-respecting people in the more fortunate classes who would rather earn their living by honest labor than get it by tricky trading or sharp financiering, or professional philanthropy or political piracy; but we may, at any rate, expect that the proportion of the shirkers will be as large at the bottom of the social scale as in any of the superincumbent social layers.

The tendency to one-sidedness of judgment always appears in men's talk about this matter. The strenuous socialist is bound to make out that the unemployed are all industrious people, willing to bear their full share of the burdens of society; but he is quite ready to believe that the conduct of the greedy capitalist and the soulless corporation is morally defective, — that *they* are trying to get their living out of their fellow men without giving an adequate return. It might occur to him that selfishness is not confined to the upper classes; that the disposition to get the good of life without paying for it is quite apt to manifest itself among people who have no capital, and that it is a poor philosophy of life which ignores or belittles this stubborn fact.

What we could easily predict from our knowledge of human nature is abundantly verified in experience. The most careful and thorough study of the industrial conditions which has ever been made is that of Mr. Charles Booth of London; it is based on a house to house investigation of a large section of that city, and it gives us a well-considered classification of the inhabitants. Mr. Booth finds that the criminal class comprises about one and a quarter per cent. of the population; and that the lowest class of those who are not habitual criminals — those who subsist on occasional labor and charity — comprises about eleven and a half per cent. of the population. This class he thus describes: —

"From whatever section Class B is drawn, except the sections of poor women, there will be found many of them who, from shiftlessness, helplessness, idleness, or drink, are inevitably poor. The ideal of such persons is to work when they like and play when they like; these it is who are rightly called the leisure class among the poor, leisure bounded very closely by the pressure of want, but habitual to the extent of second nature. They cannot stand the regularity and dullness of civilized existence, and find the excitement they need in the life of the streets or at home as spectators of or participators in some highly colored domestic scene."[1]

Such is a dispassionate estimate of a class which this high authority estimates at a little more than eleven per cent. of the population of East London. From this class the unemployed are, of course, largely recruited. The figures refer to the working-class district of London,

[1] *Labour and Life of the People*, i. 43.

and the proportion would not hold good of the whole metropolis, nor of the entire population of any American city. The percentage would be much smaller. But the existence of the class is scientifically ascertained.

Another investigation has been made in England, the results of which are thus described in a newspaper report: —

"Confessedly the most serious and the most difficult social problem relates to the unemployed. So overwhelming are the difficulties that some investigators despair of a solution amid existing conditions. Numerous expedients for special emergencies have been tried, but they have been temporary, and have only partially met the case. Charitable associations, labor unions, and municipalities have also grappled with the problem with discouraging lack of success.

"In view of these facts the results of the late thorough and scientific investigation in England are not pleasant reading. Nearly two years ago, at the suggestion of Sir John Gorst, the Toynbee Trust took the matter up, and has made the investigation of these social failures through university settlements. Twelve districts were selected: Glasgow, Liverpool, Manchester, Cambridge, Oxford, Birmingham, Sunderland, Bristol, Nottingham, Bethnal Green,

Whitechapel, and Shadwell. The results of the inquiry show that men are going from skilled to unskilled work, but not one man has succeeded in adapting himself to any skilled work with which he was not familiar. Half of the unemployed would refuse to go to the country if they had a chance. As to characteristics observed, the committee say the most striking is stolidity. Instead of finding the reckless, versatile class of popular imagination, the figures reveal a stratum of dull, apathetic men, passively resisting all outside assistance. They never go in search of work; as a class they never hear of new work. If out of work, they depend for their hand to mouth existence upon their wives and children, or upon charity, until employment is brought to their doors. They are not unemployable, but, being at the bottom of the scale, they are naturally the first to be dismissed and the last to be taken on again. It may be said, therefore, truthfully, that they neither will nor can work out their own salvation. The problem remains how to get at them for their relief and true elevation."

Such are the facts revealed by thorough investigation into the conditions of the unemployed in England. They are paralleled in this country, as we shall presently see. It must not, however, be inferred that all those who, at any time, are out of work belong to this class. In seasons like the present, of great industrial activity, the unemployed are almost wholly of this class; but there are many years, in this prosperous country, when the labor force is not wholly utilized, and when willing workers find it very hard to obtain remunerative employment. One who has been a city pastor for many years, and has spent days and weeks in vainly trying to obtain employment for industrious people, finds it hard to be patient when optimists assert that there is always work in this country for those who are willing to work. The fact is that, for the greater part of the time, the supply of labor exceeds the demand; it is only in exceptional times like the present that the surplus labor is all taken up.

In a discussion by Colonel Carroll D. Wright, the head of our National Bureau of Statistics, of the figures of the census of 1890, he estimates that during the year of that census about one twentieth of the entire labor force of the country was unemployed, — a total of 1,139,672. That was a fairly prosperous year. In the great industrial depression of 1893–94, reports from many cities showed that from one tenth to one third of all the wage-workers were out of employment. In hard times, therefore, this problem of the unemployed is a very serious one, and even in average times it demands our sympathetic attention. If five per cent. of those employed in gainful vocations are out of work in what we call good times, this fact constitutes a problem to which all men and women of good-will should give careful study. It is true, of course, that a considerable portion of those who are thus living in enforced idleness do not become a charge upon the community. Some of them have friends on whom they may depend for subsistence for a longer or shorter period; some of them are able to obtain credit of the landlord, the grocer, the butcher, the coal dealer, the boarding-house keeper. If they do not succeed in obtaining work, these debts remain unpaid and are charged up to profit and loss by their creditors, — making it necessary for these creditors to obtain larger rates and larger profits from those who can pay, and thus distributing some portion of the burden over the whole community. If they do succeed in obtaining work, these debts remain as an incumbrance, and lessen their future expenditures for the comforts of life. But some good portion of the million or more who are unemployed do thus succeed in living without making direct appeal to the cities or the charitable societies.

Just what percentage of the unemployed become a charge upon public or private charity, nobody knows. It is sufficient to say that from decade to decade an increasing number of such persons is thus becoming more or less dependent. And the first thing to be done for these persons is to find some way of separating those of them who are willing to work from those who are determined to live without work. This is the last thing that the shirkers will consent to have done. It is for their interest to prevent this discrimination. They all profess to want work; they are all looking for work; that is their occupation; they get their living by looking for work — and failing to find it; if one of them should find work, his ordinary means of livelihood would fail. It is difficult for most of us to distinguish between those who are looking for work with the hope of finding it and those who are looking for it with the hope of not finding it. The distinction is purely psychological, and none of us is omniscient. In the worst times the test of success cannot be applied, for the man who wants work then is not much more likely to get it than the man who does not want it. Nevertheless, the *crux* of the whole business is the separation of these two men. We cannot deal with either of them equitably until we know which one wants to work and hates to be dependent, and which one hates to work and would just as lief as not be dependent.

How shall these classes be separated? Some kind of work test must be devised, and it must be an adequate test, — one that can be intelligently and impartially applied. If aid of any kind is to be furnished by the town or the city, the test must be applied by the public authorities. The state or the city must have some means of finding out whether or not able-bodied persons asking relief or assistance are willing to work.

We often have work tests of various kinds connected with private charities, but these are not apt to be satisfactory. Applicants for aid are not obliged to submit to them; they may turn away from them to the public authorities which have no tests to apply; and thus the court of last resort is a tribunal that really asks no questions. Where this is the case, there is no check upon imposture.

If you have a private charity which requires all able-bodied applicants for aid to work for what they receive, that private charity is perfectly certain to get a bad name among the unemployed. Whether it deserves it or not, it will be distrusted and discredited among the poor. Those who do not want to work for their living will, of course, have no use for it; they will find all manner of fault with it; they will tell all kinds of tales about their own experience with it, or the experiences of others of which they have heard; they will diligently prejudice all their poor neighbors against it. Angels from heaven could not manage a private charity with a work test and not lose their reputation. From any private charity thus administered the great majority of the needy will turn away. So long as the city stands ready to give free aid with no adequate investigation, all attempts of private institutions to sift out the shirkers from the workers will prove abortive. The city itself must establish a work test and consistently enforce it. "The evidence is very strong," says Mr. John Graham Brooks, "that voluntary association alone cannot cope with the problem. The city must take part in such way as to allow competition between it and voluntary schemes. A certain steadiness and uniformity can alone be secured by municipal control."

The work test which the city sets up must be an adequate test. A stone pile is not sufficient. There are men who are willing to work, but who simply cannot work on a stone pile. They might sweep the streets; they might do some other useful work. But I think that in large places there should be two or three different kinds of work provided for men and two or three for women, and the applicants should be assigned by the officer in charge to the kind of work for which he or she is best fitted. The steady and persistent application of this test by the public authorities will gradually sift out the industrious from the idle.

So, then, brethren, you will find that one of your orthodox doctrines — that which affirms the necessity of separation between the good and the evil — is verified in the necessities of our charitable work. However it may be in the world to come, it is needful in this world to find some way of dividing the sheep from the goats. Neither can be rightly treated while we attempt to deal with them together. The winnowing fan is one of the indispensable appliances of good social administration. I do not say that this separation of the shirkers from the workers is to be final; the expectation is quite otherwise; you may find that in your theology, but my sociology gives no warrant for it; the separation is temporary and provisional, but it is necessary for purposes of discipline.

Having divided the sheep from the goats, what shall be done with the sheep? The work tests, of which we have spoken, should be adequate for their temporary relief. The employment offered should be such as will suffice for the frugal maintenance of those accepting it, and it would doubtless be wise that the compensation should be in provisions rather than in money, and that it should be distinctly less than that which capable workmen are able to earn in good times. There ought to be no encouragement to dependence on the public for employment. This is emergency relief; it is intended to help these industrious people through a period of stringency, and it ought not to release them from the need of vigilance and enterprise in finding for themselves suitable employment when the industrial machine is again set in motion.

It will be well also, if the employment offered by the city can be, as far as possible, work on public account, — labor upon improvements or repairs for the city itself, — so that it shall interfere no more than is necessary with the private enterprises in which laborers are at the same time earning their living.

With these safeguards, the temporary provision of work for the industrious unemployed by the town or the city is a safe and wise policy. The labor of such people will be worth what it costs; the community will suffer no loss; it will be possible to utilize their service in ways which are productive and economical. But, however this may be, it must be more economical and more humane and more Christian to find work for them than to pauperize them. If private enterprise and private capital can find employment for the multitude that is standing idle in the market-place, by all means let it be done; but if they cannot, then let the state organize for them employments by which they may eat their own bread, and know that they are giving full measure for what they receive, and are not dependents on public or private charity.

Four ways of helping the industrious unemployed can be thought of.

1. Private persons, their neighbors, or representatives of the churches or charitable societies may assist them in finding work by which they may support themselves.

2. By such private agencies alms or gratuities, in the form of money or food or fuel or clothing, may be bestowed on them, by which they are enabled to live for a longer or shorter period without work.

3. The public authorities of the city or the township or the county may furnish them gratuitous assistance in the same way.

4. The public authorities may furnish them temporary employment by which they may earn their living.

Of these four methods the first, in my estimation, is the best and the last is the second best. The other two are not to be tolerated. Neither on public nor on private charity should any able-bodied man or woman be compelled or permitted to subsist. Private charity is less demoralizing than public charity, because it is apt to be more discriminating and less degrading; but it is an indignity and a wrong to ask anybody who is willing to work to accept a dole and to live upon the labor of others. For the lack of proper organization and administration of public or private measures of relief I have often been compelled to do this very thing, but it hurts me to bestow alms on able-bodied persons, because I know how much it hurts them to receive it. But this is what the public authorities are doing all the while. When the state steps in to care for those who are out of work, whether in good times or in bad times, its assistance almost always takes the form of alms. And it takes this form because it is supposed to be dangerous for the state or the city to furnish work. That, we are told, would be a socialistic proceeding. But the state and the city do raise money, hundreds of thousands of dollars, by taxation, and bestow it as alms on able-bodied men and women. This is not socialism, but it is something much worse. Of all the ways of relieving want, this is by far the worst. It is time that this mischievous business of making paupers came to an end. And I hope, my brethren, that you may be able, in your day and generation, to do something toward putting an end to it. We are living now in a day of almost unexampled prosperity, but we must not imagine that it is permanent; the days of depression are sure to return, and you will find yourselves in the midst of multitudes who are willing to work, but whom no man will hire. When such conditions arise, it is the business of the public authorities to organize some methods by which these people may be able to earn their living by their labor. That may be socialism, but it is not pauperism. And if we must choose between the two, I, for one, find no difficulty in making the choice. All-of-us must see to it that None-of-us who wishes to work or is able to work shall be compelled either to starve or to eat the bread of charity. That is as nearly fundamental as anything can be in social theory. The injury which might come to the state through the establishment of such a claim is slight, compared with the injury which it is now suffering through the establishment of the pauper's claim. Men cry out in alarm at the assertion of "the right to work," but they seem to be quite willing to concede to increasing multitudes the right to live without work. Which involves the greater peril to the state?

What treatment, now, should be provided for those who have been proved to have a constitutional aversion to industry, who are determined to get their living without work? Such persons are social parasites. They have forfeited, by their unsocial conduct, their freedom. They have chosen not to do their part in bearing the burdens of society, but rather to impose themselves as burdens upon society. Society must therefore put them under a discipline which shall bring them to a better mind. For persons of this class workhouses should be provided, which should be not merely places of temporary detention, but training-schools of industry. It is doubtless better to regard these rather as educational than as penal institutions, because people of this class do not need to be humiliated and degraded; they need rather to be inspired and encouraged. Probably most of them deserve pity more than censure. Perhaps a few months of wholesome diet, regular habits, and intelligent direction of their thought and action may greatly improve their physical and mental condition. I do not mean that they will submit to this regimen without compulsion; it will be necessary to convince them that the discipline is not to be shirked; but the constant effort should be to arouse their self-respect and awaken their hope. The steady and resolute purpose should be to make men and women of them. If they are thoroughly trained in some kind of industry and encouraged to believe that they may become useful and self-supporting

THE STATE AND THE UNEMPLOYED 83

members of society, some of them, at least, may be rescued from pauperism. To this end the sentence to the workhouse should be indeterminate, and the discipline should not be relaxed until the subject shows good promise of reformation, and some one appears who will be responsible for giving him work in the outside world.

With these workhouses in the cities farm colonies should also be coördinated. Many of these persons would be far better off in the country; they could be best fitted for self-support by training of that kind. Not a few of them came from the country, and know more about agricultural work than about any other form of industry. It would be easier for them to find their way back to self-support in that calling than in any other.

Respecting the need of some such measures of isolation and discipline for persons of this class, let me quote from an article by Mr. John Graham Brooks, whose knowledge of this subject is wide, and whose sympathy with the needy and the unfortunate is deep and true: —

"The final question remains. What of the tramp and all his kind, whose pretense of seeking work is but a form of begging? What of those who have been offered work and have refused it? To the extent that public opinion can be slowly won to it, I see but one answer. All such must be put upon a penal farm colony or into a training-school, but in either case as much under restraint as if they were in prison. There shall be, however, this difference, that they shall be given an absolutely fair chance to work their way out by proving two things, — first, that they can do something useful, and second, that they will do it. If they continue to refuse both, then there is more reason why they should be kept under restraint than in the case of an insane person. Socialists affirm that society is to blame for the tramp. This is possible, but it is not a question of blame, but of social danger. I submit that the most superficial study of the tramp question and that of the chronic beggar, generally, in their effects upon social life, leaves no doubt that, in any kind of handling of our problem, so long as they are mixed bewilderingly together with the worthy and the hopeful, — those, I mean, who have at least good-will, and for whom something can be done, — so long as nine tenths of the citizens cannot in the least distinguish between these hopeful elements on the one hand and the despairing ones on the other, — we are blocked from taking even the first steps toward a rational dealing with this problem of charity and the unemployed. This deadbeat crowd, by any test that we can apply to it, is our greatest plague. Indirectly its expense is incomparably greater than all the disciplinary measures I am proposing. But when this crowd is considered in its relation to that part of our population which furnishes us the constant stream of the undervitalized and unfit, we see that no real gain is possible until these sources of our troubles are reached. The three great passions — the sexual, gaming, and drink — are furnished in our cities such occasion for mischief as the world has not seen. The brothel, gambling, and the saloon are organized into such formidable enticements, and are on so vast and various a scale, that they work in the deadliest conceivable way upon this class which makes our difficulty. Here the stuff for charity and the unemployed is manufactured as cloth in a mill. What a comment upon our intelligence that Massachusetts should allow 8000 feeble-minded girls to be loose in the community breeding their kind, instead of humanely and kindly shutting them up. The tramp and the professional beggar in every form is quite as distinct a danger to society, and as fruitful of results for charity and the unemployed."

We sometimes say that society is an organism, and there is truth in the biological analogy if we do not press it too far. A man is an organism *plus* intelligence and will, and so is society. The intelligence and will of the man are put in charge of the physical organism, and the intelligence and will of society are put in charge of the social organism. If the man's intelligence finds that morbid conditions have been set up in any portion of his body, he proceeds to deal with them by remedial measures. This may call for severity, for the administration of bitter medicines, for the application of heat and counter-irritants; it may even demand surgery — the free use of the knife — the excision of the diseased parts of the body. Now just as the free intelligence of a man applies the necessary curatives to his body when it is diseased, so the free intelligence which is responsible for the social organism must apply the necessary curatives to those portions of society which are morbidly affected, even though this may involve pain and suffering. And there may be, in this treatment, something analogous to conservative surgery. Not that the amputation of the diseased members of society is to be considered. No portions of the social organism are to be cut off and cast as rubbish to the void. That is not our prerogative. But the morbid elements may be separated from the social organism, not to be consigned to destruction, but to receive curative treatment, that they may be restored to their place and function in society. We separate from society in this way the criminal classes, so called, that they may be reformed. They are rightly regarded as diseased social tissue, and we isolate them that we may make them whole. All our treatment of them must have this end in view. And the same treatment must be given to the class which is sinking into penury and pauperism. Chronic mendicants must be separated from society and the sexes from each other, so that the race of "ne'er-do-weels" shall not be propagated, and so that those segregated may be reclaimed and fitted for social service.[1]

All this is the imperative social demand, to which we must give due heed. But for you and me, my brethren, there is another and a deeper motive which must never be obscured. It is not merely the protection of society, it is the salvation of these people themselves that we are to keep before our minds in all this discipline. The tramp and the professional beggar is our brother; he is worth saving, therefore we must stop pauperizing him and put him under influences that will tend to reclaim and restore him to manhood. It is the recognition of this high

[1] See a fuller discussion of this phase of the question in *Bibliotheca Sacra*, vol. lvii. pp. 135-153, "The Cure of Penury."

responsibility on the part of the state for which
I am pleading. This is work which cannot be
done by private agencies. It involves a measure of compulsion which only the state can
exercise. And the state can never do it as it
ought to be done until it gets a new conception
of its function as the representative of the divine
power and the divine goodness.

The application of the work test will reveal
to us another class for whom some provision
must be made. It will show us a considerable
number who are not unwilling to work, but who
are utterly incompetent. There is no kind of
useful industry in which they can earn their
living. If they get employment they do not
keep it, because their work is worth so little.
For these — especially for the younger ones
among them — other trade schools, not penal in
their administration, should be established, —
schools in city and country in which their hands
and their brains may be trained to do something
that may be of service to the community. Mr.
Brooks, who carefully watched the experiments
in the winter of 1893-94, in which work was
furnished by the cities to those out of employment, testifies, in the article before quoted, that
among the great majority of those applying for
relief there is "an appalling lack of even the
beginning of any kind of skill. The skilless

workman in this age of highly developed industry is, especially in cities, at a terrible disadvantage. He can produce nothing for which market value exists, nothing for which there is a real want." What shall we do for this man? We must do one of two things. We must feed him as a pauper and let him live in idleness, or we must try to teach him some kind of industry by which he may earn his living. It is a stupendous and costly blunder to let him become a pauper, and the other course is the only one that is open to an intelligent and humane democracy.

A late and inadequate remedy this must be confessed to be. The training of these people ought to have begun earlier. Our systems of education ought to make large provision for instruction of this kind. There should be a better chance for our boys and girls to learn the arts of industry. The stream cannot be thoroughly cleansed unless we begin at the fountain-head.

To this entire question of unemployment and charity a great deal of very earnest study has been given during the past twenty-five years, and you will find men and women everywhere, some in public office and some in private station, who are doing what they can to enlighten the public upon these matters and to rectify the defects of public administration. Yet there is still a vast amount of ignorance and carelessness and fatal foolishness in our handling of these difficult problems. No man can know what I have been obliged to know about the deadly effects of the pauperizing methods which the state is constantly practicing without feeling that something must be done to put an end to them. The money wasted in this bad administration is a vast sum, but that, after all, is a trifle compared with the waste of manhood and womanhold which it entails. When I see the fibre of character slowly decaying under these influences; men and women gradually losing self-respect and independence, and learning to rely more and more on alms and doles; losing the habit of thrift and living literally from hand to mouth; when I see children, by the thousand, growing up in homes where this chronic mendicancy is the rule, my heart cries out against the carelessness which permits such degradation. We have no right to allow this moral infection to spread. If we do not know enough to stop it, we do not know enough to rule this country. The pains of hunger call forth our sympathy; we ought to shield our unfortunate neighbors from that suffering; we must make sure that no one who is willing to work shall suffer hunger; but, after all, the dry rot with which hundreds of characters are stricken through, as the result of our reckless and corrupting charities, is far more terrible than any physical pain. Who of us would not sooner see any one dear to him die of starvation than sink into that abject condition where he would rather grovel as a mendicant for bread than earn it by honest work?

And you can think for yourselves — I will not try to assist your reflection — what sort of citizens these must be; what relation they are likely to sustain to bosses and boodlers; what safety there is for free government in a population containing a large infusion of such elements.

As it is through bad civic administration that these mischiefs have grown, so it must be through good civic administration that they shall be corrected and prevented. Is it not evident that the people everywhere, in the city, the county, the state, have on their hands some large and serious tasks? The business of governing this country is becoming a very intricate business, requiring the ripest wisdom, the broadest sympathy, the keenest insight into the values of character, the utmost docility under the teachings of experience, the greatest firmness in holding fast to eternal principles. For such affairs as we have been considering, what clear-minded, stainless, magnanimous men we need!

What prospect is there that the people will find such men and put them in charge of these difficult undertakings? Is not this the fundamental trouble — that the people's standards are not so high as they ought to be; that they do not rightly value the essential qualities of character? The real reason why the workingman ought not to be permitted to eat his bread in idleness is that this dependence costs him his manhood. But your political spoilsman, who is likely to be chosen to manage this business of poor relief, is himself seeking to become a pensioner or dependent on the government; he has no sense of the workingman's peril; the pauper's motive and his own are essentially the same; how can he deal with a problem so vitally involving the integrity of men? And if the spoilsman's methods and purposes are not abhorrent to the people who elect him, how can they understand the perils of pauperism?

Believe me, brethren, there is need of a radical change of heart, on the part of the great multitude of the voters, those in the churches as well as those outside the churches, in order that we may deal wisely and savingly with these great interests. The work before us — let us never forget — is the work of saving men. To this work the state is summoned. I said in my last lecture that the ministry to the poor in their homes is too sacred and personal to be performed by public officials; yet here is work which the state must do, and which can only be well done by those who have some deep sense of spiritual realities. Is it not evident that citizenship is a serious vocation? Has the Christian minister any responsibility for bringing this truth home to the consciences of the people?

IV

OUR BROTHERS IN BONDS

Of those who are described as the criminal classes, — those who are in prison, or going thither, or departing thence, — we are to speak at this time. Criminology, the study of those who have fallen under the ban of the law; penology, the study of prison discipline, are fruitful topics of investigation for students of society. The subject is one with which the Christian church and the Christian ministry ought to be concerned. No matter where your ministry may be exercised, the problems growing out of the existence of a criminal class are sure to be brought home to you. You may not have, as I have, a great penitentiary within the sound of your church bell, but men and women in every community in which you live will be going to prison, and returning from prison; and the question respecting the causes that send them thither and the influences that surround them there will be one that will force itself upon the consideration of every thoughtful follower of

OUR BROTHERS IN BONDS 95

Jesus Christ. Moreover, if no great prison is near your home, you are pretty sure to be in the immediate neighborhood of a jail or a workhouse, and some of the most serious questions connected with our penal systems in this country are those arising out of the conditions of our county jails and city prisons. There are sufficient reasons, therefore, why you should seek to keep yourselves informed respecting all the phases of this most vital branch of social study. You are sure to have opportunities of influencing public opinion and of guiding public action in a matter which deeply concerns the welfare of the state.

When we speak of crime and criminals, definitions are needed. "Crimes are wrongful actions, violations of the rights of other men, injuries done to individuals or to society, *against which there is a legal prohibition, enforced by some appropriate legal penalty.*"[1] Offenses which the state undertakes to punish are crimes. These are technically divided into felonies and misdemeanors, — the line of division between which is not very clearly drawn. Perhaps the usual distinction would be this, that a felony is an offense punished by death or imprisonment in a state prison, while a misdemeanor is an offense punished by a fine or an imprisonment

[1] *Punishment and Reformation*, by J. H. Wines, p. 11.

in a jail. The greater crimes are styled felonies and the lesser misdemeanors. Nothing, however, is regarded as a crime but that which the law undertakes to punish; a criminal is one who has fallen under the punitive prohibition of the law.

The category of crimes is therefore a shifting and indefinite one; it changes as ethical standards change, and as new conceptions of right and wrong register themselves in statutes. In days long past, deviations from the established religion were punished as crimes. The history of criminal law is full of curious illustrations of what men have thought it needful to put under the ban of the law. The German printers who first appeared in Paris with printed books found themselves denounced as sorcerers, and to escape being burnt alive, fled the city. "The Ionians," says Mr. Wines, "passed a law exiling all men who were never seen to laugh. The Carthaginians killed their generals when they lost a battle. Pliny relates that they condemned Hanno for having tamed a lion, because a man who could tame a lion was dangerous to the liberties of the people. In ancient Rome play-actors were deprived of citizenship. By the Julian law celibacy was a crime. In Sparta confirmed bachelors were stripped in midwinter and publicly scourged in the market-place."[1]

[1] *Punishment and Reformation*, p. 18.

The catalogue of obsolete crimes is a long one. On the other hand, the new social and economic conditions are greatly increasing the number of misdeeds which the law forbids and punishes. "In a word," Dr. Wines concludes, "crime is a variable quantity. It is the product of the aggregate social conditions and tendencies of a people at a given moment in its history. Actions which in one age are regarded as heroic, and which have elevated their authors to the rank of the gods, in another bring the same daring spirits to a dungeon or the gibbet."[1] In a great debate in a religious assembly, early in the last century, a speaker replied to some strictures on slavery by admonishing the critic that Abraham, who was the friend of God and the father of the faithful, was a slaveholder, whereupon Dr. Leonard Bacon arose and said: "Mr. Moderator, if Abraham were living in Connecticut to-day, we should send him to the penitentiary!"

Not merely the definition of crime changes, but the methods of dealing with it are also constantly undergoing modification. In the history of penology all the earlier chapters are chapters of horrors. Death by all manner of diabolical inflictions, mutilation, tortures, shameful exposure, everything that the ingenuity of man could

Punishment and Reformation, p. 23.

invent to produce pain and suffering, has been resorted to as the legal retribution of wrong-doing. It would not now be profitable to repeat this terrible record. In our own time the more brutal and violent forms of punishment are almost universally abandoned; the branding-irons, the whipping-post, the pillory have disappeared; in most of our states the death penalty is still inflicted, though often by methods less painful and revolting than those formerly in use, and the form of punishment for crime which has supplanted almost every other is imprisonment.

It may, however, be a fact unfamiliar to some of you that the prison, as a penal institution provided by the state, is a recent contrivance. Something of the nature of the prison existed in antiquity, but it was not a place in which men who had been tried and adjudged guilty were confined as a punishment for crime. If you will reflect upon the Mosaic sociology, with which you are of course familiar, you will remember that no mention of prisons is found in the penal laws of Moses. "In the New Testament and in Greek literature," says Mr. Charlton T. Lewis, "there is an occasional reference to imprisonment, but the word for it in Greek is precisely the word for bondage. It means to take a man and put him in chains, to fetter a man, when it is necessary to restrain him. The

Romans cast some of the apostles in prison, but for what purpose? Did they attempt thus to punish them? Such an idea never entered their minds. Every prisoner was detained for a definite purpose. He was held for trial, or to keep him out of the way of somebody who was his enemy; but imprisonment inflicted by law for crime did not exist. Prisons existed in the Middle Ages, but they were a sort of appendage to feudal power. Noblemen with castles always had prisons in them. Kings had prisons into which they could throw their prime ministers or wives or anybody they could get hold of and keep them until they saw fit otherwise to punish them. But the idea of imprisonment as a penalty had not dawned upon the world."[1]

It was not until the eighteenth century that prisons began to be used for strictly penal purposes. Men were revolting from the inhuman penalties, and in their reluctance to inflict them the criminals were left for longer and longer periods in the place of detention, and finally, the idea that the imprisonment itself was punishment enough began to get possession of men's minds, and confinement for specified legal periods was substituted for most of the barbarous inflictions which the law had formerly author-

[1] *Report of International Congress, Chicago,* 1893: Insane, Feeble-minded, and Criminals, p. 96.

ized. Doubtless it is more humane than the torture and mutilation which it has supplanted, but there is reason to doubt whether we have yet learned how to administer it so as to secure the best results.

For what reasons do we now imprison men? Imprisonment is properly considered to be a form of punishment, and our jurisprudence so regards it. One of the penalties prescribed for the violation of law is imprisonment in the jail or the penitentiary. And various reasons have been given for the infliction of the penalty. The first is the gratification of vengeance. The customary law of ancient peoples required the infliction of vengeance upon the perpetrators of wrongs or injuries. It was the duty of the sufferer himself, or of his nearest relative, to inflict an equivalent injury upon the man who had done the wrong. Private vengeance of this sort was not only regarded as a right, it was a sacred obligation; the man was execrated and despised who failed to administer it. As society became more fully organized, the lawgivers undertook to regulate this. Naturally, private vengeance tended to excesses; the retaliator rarely stopped with inflicting the amount of injury which he or his kinsman had suffered, and therefore metes and bounds were set to the exercise of this function. The Mosaic law is such an instance. "Thou shalt give life for life, eye for eye, tooth for tooth, hand for hand, foot for foot, burning for burning, wound for wound, stripe for stripe."[1] Here is, no doubt, an attempt to restrain men from excesses of vengeance; the equivalent must be exact; the injured man may take his pound of flesh, but no more. Vengeance is embarrassed, as Shylock found, when it is compelled to measure its stroke; in the care which it is forced to exercise, its fury is cooled. By and by the state in the person of its ruler took the power of inflicting punishment wholly into its own hands. It began to be dimly recognized that an injury to one was the concern of all; and that the state should protect its citizens and punish their injuries. Still, this motive of vengeance was retained as a reason for punishment, only now the punishment was not inflicted by the sufferer or his kinsman, but by the constituted authorities. That motive is still, by some jurists and moralists, regarded as one of the sound reasons for punishing criminals. I think that Carlyle somewhere says that the impulse to avenge yourself upon one who has wronged you is the foundation of our penal system. "I think it highly desirable," says Sir James Stephen, "that criminals should be hated; that the punishment inflicted upon them

[1] Ex. xxi. 23–25.

should be so contrived as to give expression to that hatred, and to justify it, so far as the public provision of means for expressing and gratifying a natural healthy sentiment can justify and encourage it."[1]

This reason for putting men in prison is one which the growth of moral sentiment has deprived of much of its force. When we consider our own inability to determine the exact amount of culpability in the case of each prisoner, and when we take into account all the facts of heredity and environment which may have contributed to lead him into the ways of transgression, we are forced to the conclusion that the cherishing of hatred toward him is a luxury in which we should sparingly indulge ourselves. We may safely conclude that the main reason why these prisoners are in our penitentiaries or our jails is not that we, the people of the state, may hate them or express our displeasure toward them, or inflict vengeance upon them.

And yet there is a proper feeling of resentment against the enemies of society. It is one of the deepest truths of the natural moral order that the way of the transgressor is hard; and one of the reasons why it is hard is that he has arrayed against himself the displeasure of his neighbors. That fact finds and ought to find

[1] *History of Criminal Law*, vol. ii. chap. xvii. p. 82.

OUR BROTHERS IN BONDS 103

expression in our penal laws. He who does wrong ought to suffer, and society ought to be so organized that he shall suffer.

We are told that the Christian law forbids retribution; that Jesus bids us "Judge not;" that he enjoins upon us the love of our enemies; that he admonishes us that vengeance belongs to God. But these words are more properly interpreted as the rule of individual conduct, and do not apply to the state which deals impersonally with evil-doers. Between my own personal feeling of resentment toward the man who has injured me and my feeling of resentment toward the enemy of society there is a clear difference. The one sentiment I cannot afford to indulge, for it may be altogether selfish; the other I may safely cherish, for it is altogether social.

Indeed, if the Apostle Paul understood the Christian law, the case is clear, for he tells us that "the powers that be" — the constituted authorities — are ordained to be a terror to evil-doers. "If thou do that which is evil," he says, "be afraid; for he [the magistrate] beareth not the sword in vain; for he is a minister of God, an avenger for wrath to him that doeth evil." The people, in a republic, are the representatives of God, and they are bound, in their methods of administration, to express the mind and will of God as best they can. They will do it but imperfectly, no doubt, but they must strive to do it. They will inadequately represent the divine justice and mercy in their attempts to reclaim evil-doers, but they must use their best endeavors. The fact that they are not omniscient should make them careful how they bear the sword of retribution, but it does not release them from the responsibility of bearing it. And it seems to me that their laws and penalties ought to express the divine displeasure against wrong-doing; that they ought to be regarded as a solemn testimony of the moral sense of the nation against those acts which tend to destroy the social order and to overthrow the kingdom of God. It is natural and right that society should regard with condign displeasure those acts which tend to make society impossible, and that it should express this displeasure in the penalties which it annexes to crime. At the same time there is great need that in the administration of punishment we learn to estimate social injuries more accurately. It is here that we are constantly making the most grotesque and mischievous mistakes. The worst public enemies of our time are not always the men who get into the penitentiary. The acts which are tending most powerfully to make society impossible are committed by men in the high places of respectability and power. There is no man in any prison in this country who has done a hundredth part as much to make society impossible as has been done by any one of half a dozen great political leaders. The man who by the corrupt use of money manipulates caucuses and conventions and debauches candidates and voters, thus poisoning at their sources the streams of political power, is the most dangerous man in society to-day; albeit his guilt is shared by those managers of great corporations who furnish him with corruption funds. If our notions of justice were clearer, such men would not be abroad in society. Compared with the destructive influence of such men, how harmless are most of the criminals shut up in our prisons. And there are other classes of malefactors with whom both law and public sentiment very inadequately deal. Such miscarriages of justice do not, however, affect the principle for which I am contending, namely, that law and penalty ought to express our moral judgment against wrong-doing, and our solemn consent to the eternal principle that suffering ought to follow wrong-doing.

In our reaction against the retributive severities of the old penology, we are in great danger of losing sight of fundamental ethical principles. Many sentimental prison reformers are in the habit of talking about prisoners, and even of talking to them, as if they were wholly innocent and amiable people, sinned against, more than sinning, rather better, on the whole, than those outside the walls. Such talk is highly pernicious. The fact that there are great scoundrels outside and undeserving sufferers inside must not lead us to minimize the wrongs which these men have done. They must be made to feel that the resentment of society against anti-social conduct is a just resentment. The first condition of genuine reform is that they shall recognize that feeling as just, and shall share it.

Nevertheless, I do not think that this ought to be the prominent motive in prison discipline. For the reasons already suggested, — because our knowledge of motives is inadequate; because it is so hard for us to judge of the real demerit of the criminal, — it is unwise to emphasize this element in our prison administration. We must recognize it as one of the motives which influence our action, but we must keep it always in subordination to other and clearer motives.

Another reason given for the imprisonment of evil-doers is the deterring not only of the criminals themselves, but of others also from the commission of similar offenses. If this were the chief reason for the punishment of criminals, it would appear that the severest and the most painful punishments would be the most effectual. This, indeed, has been the assumption until a very recent day. Not seventy years ago, the state prison of Connecticut was a cavern in the town of Granby, unlighted and unventilated, — a cave that had been excavated in mining copper ore. The passage to it was down a shaft by means of a ladder. "The horrid gloom of these dungeons," says one who visited them, "can be realized only by those who pass among their solitary windings. The impenetrable vastness supporting the awful mass above, impending as if ready to crush one to atoms, the dropping waters trickling like tears from its sides, the unearthly echoes, all conspire to strike the beholders aghast with amazement and horror." Here from 30 to 100 prisoners were crowded together at night, their feet fastened to bars of iron, and chains about their necks attached to beams above. The caves reeked with filth, occasioning incessant contagious fevers. The prison was the scene of constant outbreaks, and the most cruel and degrading punishments failed to reform the convicts. Yet no less a man than the first President Dwight of Yale College, who visited this prison on his travels through Connecticut, points to it in his published letters as an admirable prison, his approval resting largely on the powerful deterrent effect which it must have upon the minds of intending malefactors. No more humane or broad-minded man was alive in the first quarter of the last century than President Dwight; this judgment of his serves well as an indication of the change which has taken place in public opinion respecting the uses of punishment.

If it were true that the privations and severities of punishment did effectually deter men from entering upon the ways of transgression, then the state might be justified in inflicting them; it would, indeed, be a merciful thing to do. But as a matter of history, this method of repressing crime has not been found effectual. Increasing the severity of penalties has had no effect to diminish crime. In the days when penalties have been most severe and most rigorously inflicted, crime has rapidly increased. All that human ingenuity can do to make punishment terrible has been done in past generations, and the outcome of it all is recorded in the maxim, "Crime thrives upon severe penalties." Says Mr. Henry C. Lea: "The wheel, the caldron of boiling oil, burning alive, burying alive, flaying alive, tearing apart with wild horses, were the ordinary expedients by which the criminal jurist sought to deter men by frightful examples which would make a profound impression on a not over-sensitive population. An Anglo-Saxon law punishes a female slave convicted of theft by making eighty other females each bring three pieces of wood and burn her to death, while each contributes a fine besides. The Carolina, or criminal code of Charles V., issued in 1530, is a hideous catalogue of blinding, mutilation, tearing with hot pincers, burning alive, and breaking on the wheel. In England prisoners were boiled to death even as lately as 1542." Not only were these tortures practiced with a persistence which seems to us fiendish, but the death penalty, in one form or another, was dealt out with no restraint. In the sixteenth century English law punished by death two hundred and sixty-three different offenses, and as late as one hundred years ago the list of capital crimes footed up two hundred. If such stringent measures of dealing with law-breakers had no deterrent effect; if, on the contrary, crime increased under them, then the expectation of lessening the amount of crime by the severities of punishment is proved by the experience of the world to be a bootless expectation. That punishment, when reasonable and certain, does have some deterrent effect upon criminals and intending criminals is probable; but to rely on this as a main reason for punishment would be unwise.

Another reason for punishment is the protection of society. It is assumed that certain persons have become dangerous members of society, and must be confined for the security of others. The man who breaks into houses or robs stables or burns down buildings or counterfeits money or waylays passengers or assaults women is deemed a man unfit to be at large, and the law restrains him of his liberty. That society has a right thus to protect itself is not questioned. As I have said already, these are not the only dangerous people, and the day will come when we shall learn to deal with the classes that are most dangerous; but such offenses as I have described, and many others like them, warrant us in putting the men who commit them where they will be deprived of power to do harm.

But when we have got these men under our power, what are we going to do with them? Has the state — have we, the people of the state — discharged our whole duty to them when we have shut them up in a secure and not too uncomfortable place for a certain number of years as a penalty for their offenses?

"No," says the practical citizen; "that is not enough; we must make them work. It costs a good deal to keep them; they must be made to pay for their keeping by their labor.

The best prison is the prison that comes the nearest to paying expenses." But this demand may well be challenged. Even on the score of economy, there is a penny wisdom that is pound foolishness.

Suppose that our prisons are administered with a steady view to economy of administration, and with slight regard for the reformation of the prisoners. And suppose that, as a consequence, fifty or sixty per cent. of these prisoners, when released, are worse men than when they were incarcerated; suppose that they return to the ways of crime, and, after inflicting grave injuries upon society, some of which may be irreparable, are again apprehended and returned to prison. The damage which they have done while they were at large may be considerable, and the cost of arrest and trial and preliminary confinement is always heavy. Such a class of men become a heavy burden on the community.

Now suppose that, instead of administering our prisons with a view to making money out of the prisoners, we had administered them with a view to making men of them, and suppose that as a result of this treatment not more than twenty per cent. of them ultimately returned to prison; that the rest of them became industrious, self-supporting, honorable citizens, — is it not entirely conceivable that this method would be found to pay better, even in dollars and cents, than that which puts the principal emphasis on financial returns from prison labor?

But, putting aside the question of economy, there is a sacred obligation to these prisoners which is not discharged when we have kept them in confinement during their allotted terms and made them work for their living. These men are our brethren. Nothing that they have done, nothing that they can do, cancels the fact that they are the children of our Father in heaven, and that each one of us owes to them a brother's love. Jesus Christ, the Elder Brother, said, "I was in prison, and ye came unto me." By these words he identifies himself with every prisoner. By these words he bids us discern, with the eye of faith, elements of Christliness in every prisoner. In every prisoner there are divine possibilities. That is his doctrine, and it reveals our duty.

That this is the dictate of Christian love there can be no doubt. As Christian ministers, you can preach no other doctrine. As Christian men and women, we can have no other thought or wish concerning these unfortunate brethren of ours than to help them to become good men and women, honorable and useful members of society. Whatever we can do to

awaken this purpose in them we are bound to
do. If we are disciples of Him who came to
seek and save the lost, these are the hapless
ones to whom our love will first go forth.

That such should be the attitude of the whole
body of Christian people toward these unfortunate brethren is not for one moment to be
gainsaid. But what should be the attitude of
the state toward them? What should the state,
through its prison boards and prison officers
and prison discipline, undertake to do for these
people? What shall you and I, speaking in
the name of our Master Christ, bid them do?
We can have but one message for them. There
is only one law of human conduct. The state
must be simply Christian in its treatment of
prisoners. Can it set before itself any other
or lower purpose than this, to reclaim them, to
make men of them, to restore them to the ways
of useful citizenship? It seems to me that very
slight reflection will make it clear that the state
can entertain no lower aim than the reformation
of these prisoners. Any other policy would be
suicidal. The state depends for its existence on
good citizens. Lacking these, it ceases to be.
Whatever else it produces, this one product it
must not fail to secure. Its system of education is directed to this end. It cannot suffer
the standards of citizenship to be lowered. Now

in these prisoners it finds a body of men and women whose citizenship is defective. They are here in confinement for that simple reason. They are here in the care of the state. The first business of the state, in dealing with them, must be to seek to cure the defects of their citizenship and to make them sound and safe members of the body politic. This is the dictate of self-preservation on the part of the state; to fail of this is to expose its own life to deadly peril.

Every prison, then, must be primarily a reformatory. Punishment must be ancillary to reformation. To vindicate law, to terrify offenders, to seclude dangerous persons, are secondary considerations; the main thing is to change defective citizens into good citizens.

There is, however, a considerable class of penologists in these days who deny that any such thing is possible. Criminals, as a class, they maintain, are born criminals and cannot be otherwise; crime is due to some organic malformation or other; the shape of the skull and the character of the convolutions of the brain, and other such anatomical and physiological conditions determine the man's character. Thus Dr. Wines summarizes these speculations: —

"Among the anatomical peculiarities noticed

by students like Lombroso, Ferri, Benedikt, and many others who might be named, are the shape of the skull, including cranial asymmetry, microcephalism, and macrocephalism. A very frequent defect is insufficient cranial development, markedly in the anterior portion. A receding forehead is common. Criminals are said to have a disproportionate tendency to the sugarloaf or pointed head. Lombroso makes much of the unusual depth of the median occipital fossa. This is observable in the skull of Charlotte Corday, belonging to the collection of Prince Roland Bonaparte, which was exhibited at the Social International Congress of Criminal Anthropology at Paris in 1889, and gave rise to a somewhat heated discussion of the question whether she was in fact a criminal or a patriot. The same authority calls attention to the exaggeration of the orbital arches and frontal sinuses. Thieves are said by one criminologist to have small heads and murderers to have large heads. . . . The shape of the skull affects the countenance in which have been observed certain deformities of the nose and ear, peculiarities in the coloring of the eye, irregularities of the teeth, prominence of the cheek-bones, elongation of the lower jaw, and the like. . . . The prominence of the criminal ear has been especially noted. Prisoners are said to have wrinkled faces; male prisoners have often scanty beards; many hairy women are found in prison. Red-haired men and women do not seem to be given to the commission of crime. Similar remarks might be quoted relative to the skeleton, such as that convicts have long arms, pigeon breasts, and sloping shoulders." [1]

Something may doubtless be learned from these anatomical investigations respecting the causes of crime, but it is easy to build theories on narrow inductions. What is a criminal? He is a man who has broken some human law. But suppose that the law is unjust or unnecessary. A man may in such a case be a criminal without being charged with moral obliquity; he may even belong to the noble army of heroes and martyrs. Take the case alluded to, that of Charlotte Corday. The anthropologist who thought her a low murderer proved his theory by her skull; but the others who thought her a heroine, the Jeanne d'Arc of the Revolution, or as Lamartine, in his glowing eulogy, described her, "the angel of the assassination," found it easy to show that her skull was normal. The political theories of these investigators seem to have warped their scientific conclusions. By such methods the skull of John Brown or William Lloyd Garrison would be studied by

[1] *Punishment and Reformation*, pp. 232-234.

biologists south of Mason and Dixon's line as that of a traitor, and by those north of that line as that of a patriot. It is evident that much of this reasoning about physiological peculiarities rests on a very insecure foundation.

As I have reflected upon it, one question has been forced upon me. Is it not possible that the physical defects of some of these criminals may have been the occasion rather than the cause of their misdoing? Is it not possible, at least in some cases, that their unprepossessing and repulsive appearance has led to a treatment of them by kindred and neighbors which has tended toward the development in them of unsocial tempers and habits and thus to a life of crime? Children who are so unfortunate as to be defective in appearance are apt to be made aware of the fact and to feel that they are outcasts. If such a child is sensitive and resentful, such unsympathetic and contemptuous treatment will aggravate all his bad qualities and stifle his better ones; it will be easy for him to lose the sense of social obligation and to drift into the ranks of the enemies of society. Thus he becomes a criminal, not because the shape of his head or the conformation of his countenance made him one, but because of the lack of kindness in the hearts of his fellow men.

Physical defect and malformation may have

their influence in producing criminal types, but this explanation is in great danger of being overworked. And it is well for you and me to be conservative in our estimate of the number of persons who are born criminals and who cannot be reclaimed. I believe that the number of these is small, that the great majority of men in our jails and prisons are amenable to good influences, and could be saved if we had only faith and hope and love enough to save them. If our prisons were, in the true sense of the word, reformatories; if the energies of the state were bent to the work of restoring these people to citizenship, rather than to the enterprise of making money out of them, there would be good hope of saving many of them. And this is the end at which humane and Christian sentiment must aim. This is the obligation which we must bring home to the citizens, in all our teaching. Our prisons must be transformed into reformatories. It is possible that we may have need of separate places of confinement for those who have proved incorrigible, places in which there is less resort to educational methods; but the great majority of our prisoners are young men, concerning whom no such hopeless estimate can be entertained. The assumption is that they can be reformed. To this end all the discipline of the prison must be directed.

There is need, therefore, of the most careful study of the character of every prisoner, of his history, his environment, his physical condition, his habits of mind, that the treatment, so far as possible, may be adapted to his case. The discipline of the prison should be adapted to arouse the intellect, to awaken hope and self-respect, to cultivate habits of industry, to train the eye and the hand as well as the mind, to encourage thrift and providence, to strengthen all the qualities by which a man is fitted to maintain himself honestly in the outside world.

Respecting the details of prison management there is no time to speak. There has been much discussion as to the wisdom of confining prisoners in separate cells, and allowing them no intercourse with their fellow prisoners. In such a prison every man's cell is his workshop also; the kind of labor in which he is kept busy must be some simple handicraft; in the modern systems of industrial production he cannot well be trained. There is but one such prison in this country, — that of eastern Pennsylvania, — though there are many in Europe. "The advantages claimed for this type by its advocates," says Professor Henderson, "are these: it removes the man from evil associates; it trains him as an individual; it increases the personal influence of the authorities and teachers and diminishes the influence of criminals; there are opportunities for reflection; the convict who is disposed to cut loose from the criminal class cannot be identified afterward by professional criminals and so led back into evil ways by the fear of betrayal."[1] It may be practicable to treat short-term prisoners in this way, but it is doubtful whether the best reformatory results can be wrought out in solitary confinement. The trouble with the average prisoner is that he is quite too much of an individualist; what he needs to learn is how to take his place in society. "The natural life of man," says the authority last quoted, "is in coöperation with his fellows, and a system should tend to prepare convicts for freedom."[2] Bad as the associations of the congregate prison may be, there is a possibility through them of producing better results than by the other method.

In the best reformatories industrial training is always regarded as a chief factor in reformation. Many of the prisoners are destitute of skill, and have never formed habits of industry; their primary need is the power to do some useful thing and the habit of active employment. Such training as the reformatory affords "lays

[1] *Introduction to the Study of the Dependent, Defective, and Delinquent Classes*, p. 281.
[2] *Ibid.*, p. 282.

a broad foundation for later developments of skill in special directions; it awakens the dullard to increased quickness of special activity; it helps the mathematically deficient to master form, number, proportion; and it enables the passionate and ungovernable to restrain and direct their impulses of temper and appetite."[1] The industrial work of the true reformatory takes, therefore, the character of a trade school rather than that of a factory; the output of commodities is subordinated to the production of manhood.

In the best reformatories physical training in gymnasiums is also provided, and many of the kinds of apparatus found in a sanitarium, including baths, massage, and electricity, are employed. Physical renovation sometimes proves to be a great aid in the regeneration of character. Opportunities of intellectual training are also freely offered; everything is done that can be done to awaken and stimulate the mental powers, and to create purer tastes and larger interests. Mr. Brockway sometimes playfully speaks of the Elmira Reformatory as his university, and it does indeed furnish to the inmates a great deal of sound and uplifting education.

[1] *Introduction to the Study of the Dependent, Defective, and Delinquent Classes*, p. 287.

Religious teaching of some kind is generally provided for prisons, but there is reason to fear that it is not always of the highest order. A merely technical religionism would not be of much avail; the man needed for this work is the man of deepest insight, of broadest knowledge of human nature, of largest sympathy, of finest aptitude to teach and inspire and lead. The ordinary political methods do not select this kind of man for such a place. But this much may be said, — the entire administration of the true reformatory is Christian in its motive and method; its aim is to save men. It would seem to be advisable, therefore, for us as Christian ministers to keep ourselves in closest sympathy with all such efforts; to make it clear that we recognize their essential Christianity, and to forward them by all our influence.

Upon one principle modern penologists are agreed, that of the indeterminate, or terminable sentence. The attempt of our legislatures and courts to fix the term of a sentence in such a way as to proportion the penalty to the offense — "to make the punishment fit the crime" — is generally regarded as a grave failure. The words of Mr. Charlton T. Lewis strongly express the absurdity of this attempt. "We employ our best men, educated men, highly trained lawyers of incorruptible mind and heart, the picked men of the community, to sit as judges on the bench, and there to do what God himself could not accomplish because it is a contradiction in terms. We ask them to find the just proportion between the penalties imposed and the demerit of offenses and of the men who committed them on the basis of the evidence in virtue of which they are convicted. But the testimony is inadequate. If a judge were omniscient, it would only be by defying the law which placed him upon the bench that he would dare to import into his judgment any element but that which has found its way, through the quarreling and quibbling of counsel and of witnesses, to the record. And on the basis of that, is he to sit in judgment upon the intellect, the character, the life, the future of his fellow man, and decree what his fate shall be? That is what we require of him."[1] For this reason it appears to be more rational to leave the question of the length of the term of imprisonment open to be decided by the man himself. The court might fix a superior limit beyond which the imprisonment should not extend, setting it far enough away so that there should be ample time for reformation. Within that period it should be understood that the prisoner has his

[1] *Report of Chicago International Congress of Charities, Correction, and Philanthropy*: Prevention of Crime, p. 98.

fate in his own hands. The question simply is whether he is fit for citizenship. When, by his industry, his obedience to law, his evident desire to improve the advantages offered him, he seems to be ready to take his place in society and to be a peaceable and useful citizen, then, and not till then, he should be permitted to go forth. The prisoner's record, carefully observed, should furnish the basis on which he is judged. If he has become a sound citizen, the prison is no place for him, and the state has no reason for keeping him there.

But the test of the prison is not adequate. Within its walls the prisoner is safe from many temptations; no matter how exemplary his conduct may be under those restraints, we can hardly tell whether he can stand alone until he has been tried. Therefore it is needful to couple with the terminable sentence the parole system. "According to the principle of the best modern legislation," says Professor Henderson, "prisoners may be discharged conditionally before the expiration of the maximum term of their sentence, if their former lives and their behavior in prison warrant the privilege. The prisoner is permitted to go free on his parole, on his promise to avoid evil associations and haunts, to follow his calling regularly, and to report at certain stated intervals. He should not be released until a place is found for him to work, for idleness and want will lead him straight back to crime. The employer or other responsible citizen or officer is asked to confirm his report of good conduct. At the end of his term of sentence, or even before, he may be discharged from surveillance, upon the recommendation of the superintendent. If the convict violate his parole and fall into vicious and criminal ways, he may be arrested and returned for further incarceration and discipline."[1]

It must be admitted that even this method is liable to abuses. No method can be insured against them. Unscrupulous and corrupt men in prison boards or wardenships may release unfit men. The personal influence of the friends of prisoners may be allowed more weight than the facts of the prisoner's record. Only by the greatest conscientiousness and firmness on the part of the tribunal which grants the parole, and the most intelligent and vigilant supervision of the prisoner after he is set free, can the best results be secured. But experience seems to show that this method of conditional liberation is wise and salutary. Men are stimulated and encouraged by it to form good habits, to choose safe associations, and to lead industrious and honorable lives.

[1] *Introduction to the Study of the Dependent, Defective, and Delinquent Classes*, pp. 292, 293.

Certainly, the whole effect upon a prisoner of a regimen which assumes that he is to become a good citizen, which directs all its efforts to the task of helping him to become a good citizen, and which sends him out into the world with the expectation and the hope that he will be a good citizen, must be better than that of a method which simply confines him, for a term of years, as a retribution for the wrong which he has done; which makes as much money out of him as it can while he is in prison, and then opens its doors and drives him out into a world which is afraid of him, without knowing or caring much what becomes of him.

By this method the care of discharged prisoners becomes part of the business of the state, and there is less need of voluntary organizations for this purpose. There will always be need, however, of the exercise of a Christian friendship toward persons coming forth from the discipline of the prison, with a cloud upon their reputation and the consciousness of the suspicion and distrust of their fellow men. As things now are, it is the expectation of the penitentiary managers that fully fifty per cent. of those serving their first term in prison will return sooner or later; the percentage of those serving their second or third term is much greater. This may seem to some clear proof that these persons are born criminals, but the explanation in the cases of many of them is much simpler. If we add to the fact of the contamination of character and the loss of self-respect which they have suffered in prison the other deadly fact that when they come out into the world they are apt to have no friends and no opportunities of self-support, that the avenues to honest thrift are generally closed to them, we shall not wonder that they fall back into the ways of crime.

A letter written by one of these men recently discharged in my own city to one who was known to be a friend of the prisoner has been placed in my hands. Part of it I will give you, in its very words. Its artless directness and pathos are more convincing than any rhetorical improvements which I could make: —

"The main reason for applying to you is that I am right now under desperate circumstances. I have honestly and earnestly searched for honest employment all over this state and other states. I don't care how hard the work is or what it may be so long as I can support myself by it, so if you know any one you can send me to with any possible show of a job, you will be doing me a great kindness and God knows I will heartily appreciate and will make it my business to show you that I heartily appreciate. It is my earnest desire to do what is honorable and right, but as my friend —— may have told you, I have been so unfortunate as to have served time in the Ohio State's Prison and this seems to keep me back. People as a rule do not want to employ an ex-prisoner. Now all I want is just one show or chance to redeem myself and show to you and those who employ me that I will be an honest, honorable man if people will only let me.

"I have been turned down so much here and there, and by some who profess to be Christian people, until I have almost lost all confidence in all people. I am a man that believes in law and order, and I believe that a man should be punished for continual wrong-doing, and I was fearfully punished for all I done, and my God knows I don't want such a horrible thing to come into my life again. I am ready and willing to do anything to escape or get away from anything that would lead me up to a return of such things; but now, see here; when a man puts forth his best efforts to get honest employment, and it is his real desire to do right and he is in need, but is turned down all around, the devil keeps digging at him, suggesting this or that, — I tell you it is a severe trial when a man is idle and in need. I am trying to escape from the works of the devil and his service, for oh my! how well I know what they are, — nothing but woe, suffering, misery, disgrace, contempt. I want to get into something better, and it does seem impossible for me to get up to that alone; I must have help, and I am sure that I am willing to lift my part of the load."

If any man or woman can listen to this cry of a struggling soul without feeling that something is dreadfully wrong here, and that we who are the servants and followers of Jesus Christ have a responsibility in the matter, no words that I could use would make the case plainer. So long as the prison system now generally in use is maintained, and the state contents itself with punishing criminals instead of reforming them, and dismisses them at the end of their term with no provision for their future, a heavy responsibility will rest upon the Christian men and women of the community for the care of these most unfortunate people. I cannot stay to indicate the ways in which this friendship can be extended; the circumstances of different communities are so unlike that it is not easy to make practical suggestions. I only lay it upon your consciences that those coming out of prison, not less than those who are in prison, are in deep need of the saving love of all who have the mind of Christ.

Turning now, for a moment, toward those at the other end of this dolorous way, those who are standing upon the threshold of a criminal career, we are in the presence of an opportunity more hopeful and an obligation more urgent. It is probable that the vast majority of those who fall under the censure of the criminal law ought not, upon their first offense, to be permitted to go to prison; it would be far better for them and for society if they could be spared this humiliation. They have violated the law, and they ought to be made to feel its power, but there are better ways of dealing with them than to shut them up in prison. Massachusetts has substituted for the imprisonment of such misdemeanants a probation system. The offender is tried, and if convicted, the sentence is suspended; he is placed under the custody of a probation officer, whose business it is to look after him and to whom he must report. "The court," says Mr. Spalding, "bids them go and sin no more, and requires its officers to see that they do so. The continuance of the probationer's liberty depends on the use he makes of it. This is not leniency. It is not mercy. It is a practical, business-like way of dealing with the criminal. The probation officer is his custodian, as much as a warden could be, and the impending imprisonment is more salutary and more restraining than actual confinement, in most cases." The prison, under the best influences, is apt to be a school of crime. First offenders, who are inclined, when they enter the place, to turn the discipline to good account, are often discouraged by the influences surrounding them. The hardened and hopeless criminals assure them that there is no use in trying to reform; that the face of society will be set against them when they go out; that they might as well make up their minds to be outcasts. Many who are sent to prison for some offense which does not represent their habitual conduct come forth from these influences far worse than when they first encountered them. The prison is to multitudes a savor of death unto death. For this reason it is greatly to be wished that first offenders might be spared these contaminating associations. It is often said that the worst use to which you can put a man is to hang him. The next worse use to which you can put him is to shut him up in prison as the associate of many who have become habitual criminals, and who are likely to draw him into the same downward road. My own strong belief is that this method of probation is likely to be largely extended; that a considerable percentage of those now incarcerated will by and by be kept out of prison, and guarded and guided into better life. A reformatory, whose methods are directed to the restoration of manhood, is far better than the ordinary penitentiary for most of these offenders; but even for those whom we commit to the reformatories it is not improbable that a large majority would win their manhood more rapidly and more securely under the vigilant tutelage of wise and kind officials, in the school of the outside world.

The one truth that comes home to us as we study this great class of social delinquents is the truth that the state, in dealing with them, has upon its hands a task of great difficulty. If it could be content with punishing criminals, that would be a comparatively easy matter. But reclaiming them, saving them, making men of them, is quite another thing. How plain it is that for this great service we must have men of the highest and strongest character. The warden of a prison, the superintendent of a reformatory, ought to be the best man in the state. The highest are not too high, the wisest are not too wise, for this sublime undertaking. "Honest he must be," says Dr. Wines, "and kind, for if not kind, he is apt to be lacking in personal bravery. But if he is to be the centre and mainspring of educational and reformatory influences, he must be unsurpassed as a teacher and an example of purity. The work of uplifting the degraded is one which calls for the highest qualities of soul and brain. It is a work which it would not have shamed Phillips Brooks to have undertaken at Charlestown or Concord, and until we have the best men in this position we cannot hope for the best results. When the personal fate of a thousand or fifteen hundred men depends on the application to duty, the insight, the moral honesty of another man clothed with almost despotic power, it will not answer to give that power into the possession of one who does not understand his responsibilities or who is unequal to them." [1]

Consider, also, what it means to put the whole force of an institution devoted to such ends into the hands of the political spoilsmen and let them ravage it every two or three years, removing every man who could have gained any qualification for his work, and filling his place with the henchman of some political boss. Could any penitentiary do the kind of work of which we have been speaking under such a regimen as this? The subjection of our prisons to this corrupt domination, the use of them as tramping grounds and camping grounds for those who make a business of politics, is itself a gigantic crime against civilization.

I have only touched, here and there on the surface, a subject too large to be discussed with any thoroughness in a single lecture. But I

[1] *Punishment and Reformation*, pp. 227, 228.

hope that I have enabled you to see that it is a subject which the Christian church and the Christian minister cannot ignore. The disciples of Him who came to seek and save the lost have no more urgent business on their hands than that of ministering in his name to his brethren in prison.

V

SOCIAL VICES

We are to study at this time three prevalent forms of social vice: what is known, by eminence, as the social evil, the gambling mania, and the curse of drunkenness. It is evident that the Christian pulpit cannot ignore these portentous forms of social disorder. There is no community, however rural or remote, in which their ravages are not found; there is no congregation, however select or sheltered, in which their baneful influences are not felt. The work of salvation, as it will present itself to you in your ministry, in its practical aspects, will be, quite largely, the work of rescuing men from the bondage of these vices, and protecting them against their insidious temptations. Some of the most pathetic appeals to which you will ever listen will come to you from men and women, beaten and humiliated and hopeless in their struggle with these forms of evil habit, begging you to tell them what they must do to be saved. You have the gospel message to give them then, and nothing can supersede that. The one thing needful for every one of them is that he shall fully understand the nature of the help within his reach, — the grace that waits to give him the victory in his struggle, the blessedness of the forgiving grace, the reinforcement of his will which will come to him through the realization of the constant presence of an almighty Friend.

The gospel remedy for these social vices — the primary remedy — is the invigoration of the manhood, so that it shall be able to resist and overcome the temptation. I fear that the importance of this has been greatly underrated, of late, by social reformers. The entire stress of the demand for reform has been laid upon changing the environment, rather than upon strengthening the character. The efforts of the great multitude of philanthropic laborers in this field have been concentrated upon the problem of getting temptation out of the way of men, rather than upon the problem of equipping men to resist temptation. This has gone so far as to weaken, perceptibly, the sense of moral responsibility on the part of those addicted to vicious habits, and to make them feel that they cannot be expected to live upright lives so long as any chances of indulgence are open to them. The impression made by the popular presentation of

SOCIAL VICES

any of these reforms upon the mind of a drunkard or a gambler or a libertine would be that the community or the public officials or the purveyors of vice are to blame for his degradation; that he is a victim, more than a sinner; that there is no very loud call on him to be a man so long as there are opportunities of being a brute. It is a terrible mistake to permit any such impression to be made upon the mind of any man who has fallen into evil habits. The one thing for him to do is to stand and fight for his manhood. He is not saved by the removal of temptation. He is only saved when he becomes man enough to face and conquer the temptation. There is strength for him by which he may stand and overcome. The grace of God is sufficient for him; the strength of God is made perfect in his weakness. There is no promise that temptation shall be wholly removed. It will never in this world be wholly removed from any man's path. To make his salvation depend entirely or mainly on the removal of temptation is to expose his soul to mortal peril. And I cannot help feeling that the effect of the temperance propaganda, especially, for the last forty years, has largely been to undermine character, to disparage the moral forces, and to turn the thoughts of men away from the central truth of the whole question.

This is not to say that the environment is of no importance. It is of great importance, and we are bound to make it as favorable as we can to virtue. If we pray that we may not be led into temptation, we must do what we can to lessen the temptations that surround every man. Something can be done in this direction by law, as we shall see. We must work at both ends of the problem. The mistake of which I am speaking is a mistake of proportion, a mistake of emphasis. We have been putting the stress of our teaching in the wrong place. We have harped and hammered so constantly upon the saloon and the liquor traffic and the restrictions of law that the moral aspects of the case have been pushed far into the background, and the responsibility of every man for his own conduct, the sin of brutal indulgence, the possibility and duty of being a man, and the truth that God is able to save to the uttermost all who turn from their evil ways, have been treated as secondary and subordinate motives. They are not secondary and subordinate motives; they are primary and paramount motives; and the method of reform which reverses the divine order, and makes that least which is greatest and that greatest which is least, is bound to have disastrous consequences. The failures in our measures of social reform, so far as these vices are concerned, may be, at least in part, attributed to the faulty perspective in the popular teaching.

The mistake may be due, in part, to the aberrations of the Zeitgeist, who has been somewhat out of his head for the last generation or so, having got hold of some crazy and incomplete theories of evolution, and being inclined to regard the environment as the sole and decisive factor in the development of life. But he is now coming to himself and beginning to admit that the spiritual forces have their part to play in the great drama; and while he will never suffer us again to neglect the power of circumstance, our thought will not, I trust, be so enthralled by it as it has been during the decades just past. In the period during which you will exercise your ministry, it may be less difficult than it has been in recent years to make social reformers see that the truth which must never be minimized or blurred is the responsibility of every man for his own manhood, and his duty, in the presence of whatever hostile influences, to fight the good fight and overcome.

I. When we come to consider the nature and the magnitude of that form of vice which is known as the social evil, and the relation thereto of the Christian church and the Christian pulpit, we find ourselves in the presence of a problem which the pulpit must treat with great discretion. How much can be done by law for the abatement of this evil I do not clearly know. It seems to be a monstrous thing that sections of our cities should be overrun with this curse; that there should be large areas in which a decent woman cannot appear by night without danger nor a reputable man without suspicion. The resolute attempt of Dr. Parkhurst to abolish these plague spots was the dictate of sound moral feeling. But it is asserted by those who ought to know that these heroic measures spread the infection instead of stamping it out, and that the conditions in New York have been far worse since that day than they were before. This may have been the result of a failure to persist in this drastic treatment; it may be that a resolute and continuous effort to suppress vile houses would succeed in ridding the community of them. A recent article in the "Outlook," narrating the battle of Father Doyle and the Paulist Fathers with the social evil on the West Side of New York, seems to show that when the people of the vicinage are thoroughly aroused, and when the police authorities can be depended on, the more flagrant exhibitions of this iniquity can be prevented. But such measures can be effectual only when all sections of the city are united in the effort; otherwise the pest

SOCIAL VICES

is only driven from one ward to another, and the curse is simply shifted.

What law can do, in existing conditions, for the abatement of this evil is not altogether clear. But it seems that in civilized communities it might, at least, be prevented from flaunting its indecencies in the streets and displaying its enticements at doors and windows. I do not think that we shall have risen to a very high level of morality, when we have merely determined that the public highways shall not be the market-places of lust and shame, and that snares shall not be openly set, in the sight of every passer-by, for unwary feet. It is ridiculous to say that the plying of this accursed traffic in the streets cannot be prevented. Such open allurements exist in no city without the connivance of the police, and can be abolished in any city whenever the police authorities choose to abolish them. So much as this we may demand of the law in every community, and the accomplishment of this would be a great gain in many of our communities.

One measure, in alleviation of the injuries wrought by this iniquity, may be confidently supported by all of us, — that is, the establishment and maintenance of places of refuge in which the women and girls who are ready to abandon their evil life may be received and cared for. It is a dreadful fate in which the woman is involved who finds herself swept downward in the mad currents of this life of degradation ; to escape from it is not easy ; it is rarely the case that there are any kindred who will offer her a shelter; few decent homes are open to her; she is apt to feel, in her remorseful moments, that she has made her bed and must lie in it. Doubtless to many of these hapless children of sin there often comes a strong sense of the misery and woe of it all and a deep wish for some way out of it, but the way of deliverance does not appear. Such a door of hope ought to be opened and held open in every large city. It may be the verdict of experience that not many of those who enter upon this horrible path ever leave it until health is gone and life is blasted; but the grace of salvation is for the few even when the many refuse it, and if by any means we can save some, we must not neglect to provide a way of salvation. Such work is, I believe, more hopeful than many persons think; the experience of those who have had much to do with it gives good ground of hope. The Florence Crittenton Homes, which have been established in many cities, largely through the faith and devotion of one man, have a bright record to show of lives that have been rescued from this pit and made clean and pure. It must be remembered that many young girls are drawn into these currents almost unaware; they have been betrayed and abandoned; a place of refuge in the day of their great trouble, a helping hand held out to them just then, may keep them from destruction. For the lack of such succor in the hour when they need it most, many souls are lost.

The Christian people of every considerable community ought, therefore, to see to it that such a place of refuge is provided for those who will turn from their evil ways and live. The disciples of Jesus Christ must not forget the attitude of their Master toward persons of this class; they must not fail to remember that it is the lost that he came to seek and save.

You will find, however, my brethren, as you study this question, year after year, the conviction deepening in your minds that such checks and palliations as we have been considering hardly touch the surface of this vast social ulcer. What law can do to prevent its shameless effronteries, what philanthropy can do to rescue its miserable victims, are but slight mitigations of an enormous and growing evil. In some way we must find the sources of the evil and apply our remedies there.

What are the sources of this evil? What are the social conditions from which it naturally flows? Doubtless many causes conspire to produce it, but one, at least, seems to me of grave importance. I refer to the growing unwillingness on the part of young men to assume the responsibility of a family and of young women to take the risks and the tasks of maternity. A large number of the young people of the more cultivated classes seem to shrink more and more from family life, or at least to defer, to later and later periods, the setting up of the home. The standards of social decency and respectability are constantly rising; the amount of money supposed to be necessary to begin the married life increases decade by decade. Young men say that they will not marry until they are able to support a wife in good style, and as the wealth of the land increases and their neighbors live more and more luxuriously, the phrase "in good style" is constantly undergoing changes of meaning. Young women become accustomed in their parental homes to a certain amount of comfort and of leisure, and they do not relish the thought of beginning to live more plainly and more laboriously in homes of their own. Thus an increasing number of young men and women decline or postpone marriage. It is true that the family life does require of both men and women the relinquishment of a certain amount of liberty, the assumption of new burdens, the incurring of pain and privation and sacrifice. The unwillingness to meet these demands is the prime cause of the diminution in the number of marriages which the census reports to us. And one of the inevitable consequences is the increase of social immorality. The condition of France, a prosperous and luxurious nation, where the number of marriages is lessening and the birth-rate is decreasing, and social vice is assuming appalling dimensions, points out the path in which the nation must travel whose young men and women undervalue the family relation.

I do not believe that there is any remedy for this social disease but the restoration of a more wholesome sentiment concerning this whole subject of family life. The morality of what we call our respectable classes needs toning up all along this line. Many parents discourage the marriage of their sons and daughters under conditions which would be far more favorable than those under which they themselves set out in life bravely and happily. They are unwilling that their children should meet the responsibilities which they met and bear the burdens which they bore, and in meeting and bearing which they won their own manhood and womanhood. Many a father refuses his daughter to a young man whose circumstances and prosperity are far more favorable than were his when he was married; many a mother warns her son against alliance with a girl whose heart is as true and brave as hers was when she set up her own home. The father and mother, in their prosperity, have lost their sense of the value of character; they have come to put far too much emphasis on the mere accidents of life. For it is true not only of a man's life, but of the life of a man and woman together, that " it consisteth not in the abundance of the *things* that " they possess. They can be happy and true and brave with but few things. To begin together as their parents began, to live simply and frugally, to face the problems of life without flinching, to exercise their wits together over a limited *ménage*, what is this but the discipline in which all the best qualities of life are won?

The habitual thought of the entire community upon this subject is largely perverted by the practical materialism which prevails. The sacred function of the family is dishonored when it is made subordinate to the demands of style and the claims of luxury and of leisure. It is a good for which right-minded human beings should be willing to pay in toil and sacrifice. No great good is obtainable at a lower price; and the refusal to accept marriage and parentage on these terms is a cowardly infidelity to the highest claims, which nature is sure to punish.

I have no doubt, for my part, that this is one of the underlying causes of the prevalence of the social evil whose ravages in society we are now considering. Other conspiring causes may be found in the unsettled economic conditions, and in the transition from old to new philosophies of life, but the deeper reason is the growing love of ease and luxury, the growing subserviency to the demands of style and fashion, the growing disposition among our prosperous classes to exalt the accidents of life above its essential values. It is a subtle form of sin, but it is visited with a terrible penalty. The plague which breaks out in the purlieus is due to the atmospheric poison which is engendered on the avenues. The only effectual cure for this social ulcer is the tonic which shall invigorate the moral sense of the influential classes and teach us all that a man is more precious than fine gold, and that a home is not the product of the upholsterer.

The relation of the pulpit to this question will therefore be less obvious and immediate than to some of the other questions with which you are dealing. It will not be wise to preach about the effects, so much as about the causes. The artificial and luxurious life of our modern society is the heart of the trouble; the overvaluation of style and fashion; the undervaluation of the happiness that consists with plain and simple living; the theory that the only life that is life indeed is one that consists of an abundance of things. Whatever you can say to make young men and women see the beauty and nobility of simpler manners and quieter pleasures, the superiority of a genuine friendship to the advantages of fashionable society, the truth that the completion of life for the man or the woman lies in the love which divides our sorrows and doubles our joys, will help in the most effectual way to dry up the poisoned springs from which this stream of pollution issues.

In President Roosevelt's lecture on "The Strenuous Life" are the kind of counsels on this subject with which you will do well to fill your own souls and the souls of all committed to your charge.

"In the last analysis a healthy state can exist only when the men and women who make it up lead clean, vigorous, healthy lives; when their children are so trained that they shall endeavor not to shirk difficulties, but to overcome them; not to seek ease, but to know how to sweat triumph from toil and risk. The man must be free to do a man's work, to dare and endure and to labor to keep himself and to keep those de-

SOCIAL VICES 149

pendent on him. The woman must be the housewife, the helpmeet of the home-maker, the wise and fearless mother of many healthy children. In one of Daudet's powerful and melancholy books he speaks of ' the fear of maternity, the haunting terror of the young wife of the present day.' When such words can be written of a nation, that nation is rotten to the heart's core. When men fear work or fear righteous war, when women fear motherhood, they tremble on the brink of doom, and well is it that they should perish from the earth where they are fit subjects for the scorn of all men and women who are themselves strong and brave and high-minded."[1]

The prevalence among our more prosperous classes of such sentiments as these would have many blessed consequences; among them would be a great abatement of that social curse whose devastations we are now considering.

II. Among the social evils which have greatly diminished during the nineteenth century are the evils of gaming. Relatively to the population and the wealth of the country, there is much less gambling now than when General Washington was President. At that time it was hardly discreditable to win money by gambling or betting. General Washington freely records in his diary sums of money won or lost by him in

[1] *The Strenuous Life*, pp. 3, 4.

betting upon horse-races. The same is true of Thomas Jefferson. It would be easy to produce such evidence from the cash-books of the majority of the public men of that time. Washington's notions of propriety, as every one knows, were very strict; he kept himself from everything that would cause scandal, yet he saw nothing questionable in betting on a horse-race. The sentiment in England with regard to this particular vice is much less rigid at the present time than in this country; Lord Rosebery indulges in this form of gambling, as do many others of his class; nevertheless, Lord Rosebery suffers some loss of respect on account of this indulgence, and one of our own public men, in a similar position, would hardly risk the injury to his reputation which would be inevitable if he were suspected of any such practice. In Lord Rosebery's country, a little more than one hundred years ago, in the days of the Georges, men like Chatham, Fox, Bolingbroke, and Wilberforce were in the habit of gambling heavily, and some of the most popular clergymen of that period were known to be addicted to the same vice. Even in England the public sentiment has greatly changed for the better, and in our own country it has found clear expression upon the statute-books of most of our states in the prohibition, under heavy penalties, of all forms of gambling. Even the great lotteries, which lingered latest, and which were resorted to not very long ago for the raising of funds to build colleges and educate ministers of the gospel, have finally been swept away.

Over against these gains of morality certain losses must, however, be reckoned. The most prevalent form of gambling in these days is one unknown to our great-grandfathers. That is the gambling of our stock and grain and produce exchanges, — the gambling which constitutes so large a part of what we call trade. The difference in principle between buying and selling on margins and betting on a horse-race or a ship's progress has always been a difficult one for me to make out. I am familiar with the arguments which show how this betting acts as a regulator of the market, and how a legitimate trader may avail himself of it to protect himself against fluctuations which may occur betwixt the purchase and the delivery of goods. Doubtless certain benefits may result from it; there are few great evils which do not bring in their train some incidental gains; nevertheless, it appears to me that the net result of this system of commercial gambling is an ethical injury of no small dimensions. If I could be convinced that it is an essential part of the present system of exchange, I should be sure that the present system of exchange is radically unsound and must give place to something less hurtful to character. I am not, however, convinced that it is essential to the life of commerce as at present organized; I believe that some other method could be found of securing those ends of regulation and of insurance which stock and produce gambling are now supposed to serve.

You will find yourselves confronted in your ministry by this stupendous system of stock and produce trading, the nature and tendencies of which you will need to study thoroughly. It is a somewhat complicated question; I advise you not to be in too great haste to discuss it; make sure of your ground.

You are very likely to be brought into close contact with some of these transactions, and you will need to have clear ideas respecting the ethical principles involved.

In what we call trade there are at least three kinds of operations which need to be distinguished.

The first is legitimate trade, which consists in supplying to the consumer such goods as he needs, and in charging him a reasonable sum, in the way of profit, for the service rendered. The merchant who brings from producers, far and near, such things as I need, keeps them subject to my demand, and delivers them to me when I call, is performing for me a most valuable service, and is as much entitled to a reasonable profit on the transaction as the gardener who plants my ground is to receive wages for his work. The trader who took advantage of my necessities and made me pay an exorbitant price for goods that were indispensable to me would be an extortioner and a robber; but when the disposition exists to deal fairly and to charge no more than a reasonable profit, the business of trade is not only legitimate but beneficent. There is no reason in the nature of things why the trader engaged in a purely commercial business should not adopt the Christian law of exchange, which is simply, "Give as much as you can," — as much as you can consistently with the maintenance of the business and the securing for yourself of a reasonable livelihood.

The second of the operations included under the name of trade is what is known as speculation. This involves buying commodities or properties and holding them for a rise; buying when the market is depressed and waiting for it to recover. The gain of the speculator is made out of the fluctuations of the market. The more sudden and sharp are these fluctuations, the larger are his chances. To all legitimate business these fluctuations are highly injurious. The speculator, *qua* speculator, makes his gains, therefore, out of the misfortunes of his fellows. He does, however, render some service both to those of whom he buys and to those to whom he sells. His function is not purely that of the spoiler. But he gives less to the seller than the seller in normal times would rightly receive; and he gets more from the buyer than the buyer in normal conditions would be obliged to pay. It is difficult, then, to see how the speculator could adopt the Christian maxim, "Give as much as you can." The principle of his action requires him to give as little as he can for what he gets in every transaction. That is probably the principle on which most business is done, and it cannot be stigmatized as dishonest or wrong, when judged by the commonly received basis of commercial morality.

It must also be said that the speculative element enters more or less into nearly all legitimate trade. Most of those who buy goods or property of any kind hope that the price will rise before they are compelled to sell.

We are not, therefore, called upon to condemn speculation as essentially immoral; but it is plain that the principles on which it rests and the motives to which it appeals are distinctly lower than those which are involved in legitimate trade. Trade might be conducted benevolently, with the purpose of service as the paramount motive; speculation is guided by a purely egoistic aim.

The third operation which is included under the name of trade is gambling. That is an operation in which no goods are exchanged and no services rendered; it consists of a transfer of value from one person to another with no pretense of rendering an equivalent. It is a method of getting something for nothing by an appeal to luck or chance. Legitimate commerce consists in a fair exchange of values. If I buy goods of a merchant, there is an exchange of money for merchandise; the merchandise is worth more to me than the money, and the money is worth more to the merchant than the merchandise; both parties to the transaction are gainers. If I employ a physician to attend me in illness, or a music-teacher to give my children lessons, or a laborer to clean my carpet, there is also an exchange of values; I give my money for the services of the physician or the music-teacher or the laborer, because they are worth to me more than the money. But when one man bets another that a certain card has such a face, or that a certain horse will trot a mile sooner than another, or that wheat will bring so much in thirty days, and wins his money, what exchange takes place? The winner has got his money and given nothing for it; the loser has parted

with his money and got nothing at all for it.
The study and the purpose of the gambler, *the
gambler's business*, is to get money or other
property belonging to others and to give in exchange for it absolutely nothing. Whatever
any one wins in gambling some one else loses;
by as much as he is enriched some one else is
impoverished; for all that he has got he has
given no equivalent; other people have parted
with what he has gained and he has given them
for it no merchandise, no service, no pleasure,
no accommodation, nothing whatever.

Kant's rule applied to this transaction reveals
its nature: "Act upon principles of universal
application." If all men acted on the gambler's
principle, what would become of society? The
principle is distinctly and exactly anti-social;
the gambler's relation to economic society is
essentially the same as that of the thief. There
could be no economic society if all men followed
his rule.

This is the ethical principle which underlies
the laws making gambling a crime. It is a perfectly sound principle. I do not think that it
is generally understood. I have asked many
persons to tell me what is the essential evil of
gambling, and have very seldom received the
true answer. The evil is generally supposed to
consist in the injurious effects upon the gam-

SOCIAL VICES

bler's character, — in making him restless and feverish and indisposed to honest industry. But that is an inadequate diagnosis. The truth is that the gambler is essentially a thief; he gets his neighbor's property away from him without giving him any equivalent for it. You will need, then, to get a firm grip upon these principles, and to enforce them in your teaching, no matter whom they hit. Few questions of ethics are more important just now, or call more loudly for clear and trenchant treatment. The invasion of trade by the gambler's practices needs to be met with a distinct prophetic testimony against the essential nefariousness of the business in all its shapes and disguises.

I am told by those who ought to know that polite society is suffering the same invasion. Various games of hazard, in which money in considerable amounts is lost and won, are said to be in vogue in circles which not long ago were considered respectable. A young girl from my own city recently visited New York, and found herself in an elegant home, where a card-party with this spice for its diversion was to assemble in the evening. The girl had scruples against gambling and begged to be excused, but her hostess insisted that she must play, making her feel that she would violate the obligations of hospitality if she refused. With a great reluctance she yielded, and lost during the evening considerable money. The hostess offered, the next morning, to make good her loss, but the girl had spirit enough to refuse that reparation; since the greater wrong she had suffered could not be undone, she would not permit the lesser to be repaired. The essential vulgarity and brutality of a society in which a thing like that can happen does not need to be pointed out.

The state of mind which can find amusement in winning another person's money is one into which I find it impossible to enter. I have watched travelers, in the sleeping-cars and on the steamships, playing by the hour, for larger or smaller stakes, and apparently finding in the game, because of its winnings, a zest which without them would have been wanting. It was pleasure to get another man's money away from him and give him nothing in exchange for it! That spectacle always fills me with amazement. There is something so essentially sordid about it, that it seems to me beneath contempt. I marvel that any gentleman or lady can find diversion in playing for money. What! have we sunk, in our miserable money-grubbing, to such a depth as this, that we are forced to turn even our pastimes into schemes for gain?

If you are to be true teachers and prophets of righteousness, you will have to bear some clear and pointed testimony against this insidious and deadly iniquity. There is no doubt that in the sudden ascent to affluence of a multitude with minds untrained and characters unspiritualized, these low-lived pleasures are easily propagated. The new-rich are apt to cultivate questionable amusements. Against all these tendencies the voice of the Christian minister must be lifted up. You cannot let such vices alone. They will infest your own congregation; they will assail and corrupt the characters of your young men and women. You must do what you can to create a public sentiment which shall make them disreputable.

In many of the larger cities gambling is a business, carried on with more or less publicity, in places known to most intelligent citizens. Against the keeping of such places there is law enough, everywhere; and the law is based, as we have seen, on sound ethics. But the administration of the law in many places is extremely lax; the police authorities corruptly, either for money or political support, ignore the violation of law and permit this infernal traffic to go on. Gambling places in many of our cities are as public as the drug-stores; even the games and winnings are sometimes reported in the newspapers. Such a defiance of law ought not to be tolerated, and the Christian pulpit is responsible for arousing the moral sense of the community to demand the enforcement of the law. There is no such difficulty here as in the case of the liquor laws. The vast majority of reputable citizens are opposed to gambling in all its forms; all intelligent business men are well aware of the perils to which it exposes them, in undermining the characters of trusted employees; the only reason for the failure to enforce the laws against gambling places is found in the corruption or the inefficiency of the police authorities. An awakened public sentiment would compel these derelict officials to do their duty, or would replace them with others of a different character. But the public opinion which demands this reform must at the same time and with equal positiveness denounce and put to shame the sugar-coated gambling that is going on in the drawing-rooms of the "four hundred."

Deeper than all this your ploughshare must go, — down to the subsoil of this vice, the disposition and determination, in all our commerce with the world, to get something for nothing. That is the soil in which the gambling habit grows. A great many of the rest of us are one with the gambler in his central purpose. We

SOCIAL VICES

are glad, whenever we can, to get something for nothing; to win gain or credit or power for which we have not given and do not mean to give any fair equivalent. We are all too eager to get rich by short cuts; to receive marks which do not represent achievements; to win success by some lucky throw; we are not so willing as we ought to be to pay full price of labor and patience and prudence and frugality and fidelity for the successes that we crave. The roots of all injustice, of all dishonesty, of all heartlessness and cruelty, are in this disposition, and find in it their proper nourishment. The only radical cure for the social distemper of gambling is in the change of mind which brings the grace of contentment, the equable temper which can thrive in narrow fortunes, and not less the equitable and honorable spirit which scorns to take away any man's possessions without rendering him a fair equivalent.

III. Respecting the third and last of the social evils which we have undertaken to group in this discussion, there is so much to say that I am tempted to say nothing. The treatment which I shall give it must needs be fragmentary and inadequate. The subject, however, is one which has been so thoroughly discussed for so many years, that you are pretty familiar with all phases of it, and there is need of scarcely anything more than a few practical suggestions as to the best methods of dealing with it.

1. At the outset, let me admonish you that this is a subject in the discussion of which you will need to cultivate serenity of mind and an unresentful temper. In religious controversy most of us have learned to be fairly tolerant; we can understand that a man may differ with us on a theological point without being an enemy of the truth. This spirit does not always prevail among the earnest friends of temperance. There are many who are apt to regard all who do not agree with them as to methods as the paid agents of the saloon interest. This uncharitableness is to be deplored; it has weakened the cause of temperance. The question is really a difficult and complicated one; there is large room for honest difference of opinion as to the best methods of dealing with it; and it is desirable that many different methods should be fully and fairly tried, that we may have better reasons than our own subjective impressions for believing one method to be superior to another. It is therefore important that in all our investigations and discussions we all try to keep our tempers, and avoid uncharitable judgments. It is hard to be tolerant of intolerance; but this is one of the first lessons you will have to learn if you are going to discuss with profit the temperance question.

2. Recall what was said at the beginning of this lecture; keep the interests of character supreme and give due honor to the moral forces. Make the drunkard feel that he is responsible for his drunkenness, and that if his will is too weak to resist temptation, there is omnipotent grace on which he may rely.

3. In dealing with the question of the personal conduct of those who are not drunkards, make it clear that while abstinence, for love's sake, is the highest rule of conduct, it is of no value, as an example, unless it is self-imposed. To have any effect upon the mind of the drunkard, it must be purely voluntary, — it must not be due to the pressure upon the abstainer of public opinion. If the drunkard thinks that I am depriving myself of what I might safely and innocently use, because I want to encourage him to abstain from what he cannot use without peril, my example may have some weight with him. If he knows that I am abstaining because I am afraid of losing credit with the temperance people, it will have no weight with him at all. The man who says with Paul, "I will eat no meat while the world standeth, if it make my brother to offend," takes a noble stand. The man who says, "I am fond of meat and would eat it if I dared, but I am afraid that if I did the Anti-Meat Association would make it disa-

greeable for me," is not likely to exert a very wide influence among the meat-eaters.

4. In dealing with the question of legal regulation of the liquor traffic, it is best to be undogmatic. Many methods have been tried; none, as yet, has demonstrated its superiority. License does not appear to afford the restriction needed; state prohibition has been measurably successful in the rural districts, but a complete failure in the larger cities; the Swedish and Russian system of governmental monopoly of the traffic, which has been tried in South Carolina, can hardly be said to have justified the expectations of its friends nor the predictions of its enemies; its efficacy is still in doubt.

Perhaps we may say that the best results, thus far, have been gained under some form of local option. My own belief is that this is the method which is now most promising; and that it ought to be extended not only to townships and municipalities, but to wards or other subdivisions of cities, so that each neighborhood may determine for itself whether this traffic shall be permitted within its boundaries. All sorts of theoretical objections may be made to this method; undoubtedly it would appear to some persons a great anomaly that what was lawful on one side of a street should be criminal on the other side. But we shall show our wisdom in dealing with the temperance question if we adopt the good old Anglo-Saxon principle of fixing our eyes on practical results and letting the anomalies take care of themselves. There is a street in a small city through which I often pass, the dwellers on one side of which recognize and obey a wholly different set of laws from those recognized and obeyed by the dwellers on the other side; for the line between Ohio and Indiana runs through the middle of the street. But the people seem to get along very well together, and there is neither confusion nor anarchy. Disregarding considerations which are purely ideal, we may confidently say that such an extension of local option would result in banishing the open saloon from large sections of every great city. If the people of any ward or legislative district regard the open saloon as an injury to their property and a nuisance in their neighborhood, they ought to have the power to rid themselves of it. If those of other neighborhoods are differently affected toward it, their preference ought to be followed. Time will perhaps demonstrate whether its presence or its absence brings the greater advantage. If the traffic in which the saloon is engaged were universally regarded as essentially immoral, such an arrangement could not be defended; but the fact is that large numbers of our people consider the traffic to be entirely legitimate and beneficent, and it is impossible for the people of one section to put honest and reputable people of another section into the category of criminals upon a question of this nature.

5. To one conclusion I have clearly come, namely, that wherever it is decreed that the saloon must go, there it is the bounden duty of those who abolish it to see that something better takes its place. Most of those who have been talking about the saloon all their lives and saying many hard things about it have very little knowledge of its real character and function. But this is a scientific age, and quite a number of people have formed the curious habit of trying to find out what things are before they pronounce them good or bad. Several of these people have been investigating the saloons, — spending weeks and months in them, and carefully recording the facts which they have thus observed. It must be allowed that these reports have modified to some extent the opinion of intelligent men respecting the nature of the saloon. Speaking for myself, I can say that they have not convinced me that the typical saloon is, on the whole, a useful institution. I am still of the opinion that its influence is, on the whole, highly injurious; that it is responsible for an enormous waste of money which is needed for

the comfort and the pleasure of the families of the men who spend it; that it helps to cultivate in great multitudes habits which are destructive to health and character. I should like to see the number of drinking saloons greatly lessened, and I wish that the moral sense of the people would demand that they should be abolished altogether. But I must admit that the recent investigations have made it plain that the saloon, along with its injurious effects, does serve some useful purposes. It is probable that with the majority of those who frequent the saloons, the craving for drink is a subordinate motive. The saloon supplies "the demand for social expression;" that is a large part of its function. "The social stimulus of men," says Mr. Moore of the Hull House, who spent several months in the saloons of the nineteenth ward of Chicago, "is epitomized in the saloon. It is a centre of learning, books, papers, and lecture hall to them. It is the clearing house for common intelligence, the place where their philosophy of life is worked out, and their political and social beliefs take their beginnings."[1] Professor Walter A. Wyckoff, whose opportunities of observation have been abundant, says: "My short association with workingmen in this country gave to me a very strong impression of the perfect adap-

[1] *Economic Aspects of the Liquor Problem*, p. 226.

tation to their social needs which the saloon as an institution supplies. There is no social fact apart from the family which seems to me, by reason of its strength and efficiency, to bear comparison with the saloon in its influence upon the lives of workingmen in America."[1]

In a most instructive volume, entitled "Substitutes for the Saloon," Mr. Raymond H. Calkins thus moralizes: —

"An unbiased study of the saloon, as it exists in our American cities under many differing laws and in its many different forms, compels the conclusion that it is acting to-day as a social centre, even where this purpose is farthest from the mind of its keeper, and where its apparent attractiveness is reduced to its lowest terms. Upon closer examination the importance of this result only increases, and the real hold of the saloon upon the social life of the people becomes more and more clear. It is apparent for one thing that there are not many centres of recreation and amusement open at all hours to the working people, none that minister to their comfort in such a variety of ways. The longer one searches for just the right kind of a substitute for the saloon, affording its conveniences without its evils, the more one despairs of finding it. And yet such places are a positive neces-

[1] *Economic Aspects of the Liquor Problem*, p. 237.

sity, for the social instinct which demands and finds its satisfaction within the saloon is a reality."[1] It would be easy to multiply these witnesses. And their testimony shows that the extirpation of the saloons is not a simple problem. They ought not to be abolished without making some provision for that need to which they so efficiently minister. The subject is too large to be entered upon here; but it is now tolerably clear that the first step in the temperance reform — the obligation which precedes and outranks all others — is the invention and supply of some sort of social substitute for the saloon. This is not an easy problem. It must not be a charity; that would kill it. The workingmen who patronize the saloons want no gratuities. It must rest on an economic basis. It must be a self-supporting institution. In England a great number of Coffee Houses and Refreshment Rooms have been established all over the kingdom; they have been economically profitable, and they have proved a strong counter-attraction to the public house. In America such experiments have been few and feeble. The time has come when the practical American must grapple with this difficult problem. And it might be wise for our ardent reformers to stop denouncing the saloon-keeper long enough to

[1] *Substitutes for the Saloon*, pp. 4, 5.

get acquainted with him. One of the principal things that he is doing is the thing that they have got to learn to do. The only way in which they can get rid of him is to meet him on his own ground and beat him at his own game. He has found out how to furnish a social resort to which men like to come, in which they feel at home, where their social needs are ingeniously supplied. Before the saloon-keeper is driven out of the business, somebody must show that he can do this thing as well as the saloon-keeper does it.

"The saloon, as it appears to me," says Mr. Wyckoff, " in relation to the working class in America, is an organ of high development, adapting itself with singular perfectness to its function in catering in a hundred ways to the social and political needs of men; and if it is to be combated successfully by an institution, this institution must be rooted in natural causes and must minister with equal efficiency to real social needs.

"In view of results for which the saloon is largely responsible, in the wreck of individual lives, in the known relation which its traffic bears to the totality of crime and pauperism and insanity, and the unmeasured misery caused by the consuming appetite which it breeds, it is vital that an opposing institution rooted in the necessity of reform and in conscious responsibility for one's fellow men, and having, too, a valid economic basis in yielding profit, should be fostered by infinite patience and care, and grow in all helpfulness and practical adaptation to constructive social good." [1]

That is the temperance problem of the twentieth century. I trust that you, my brethren, and the people whom you will inspire and lead, will have some good part in working it out.

[1] *Economic Aspects of the Liquor Problem*, pp. 239, 240.

VI

PUBLIC EDUCATION

IF you had been called to exercise your ministry in New England two hundred years ago, you would have met no question respecting the relation of the church or the ministry to public education. At that time it was supposed that education was fundamentally a religious function; that the school and the church were engaged in the same enterprise. Perhaps the first public action taken in the country providing, by direct taxation, for the establishment of a school, was that of Dorchester, in Massachusetts, in 1639, and this action was taken "in consideration of a relligeous care of posteritie," and because the voters knew "how necessary the education of theire children will be to fitt them for public service both in churche and commonwealth in succeding ages." The religious motive was always avowed in connection with the establishment of public schools, and provision was made for definite religious instruction in the Bible and in the catechism. Some of us have memories that go back to the time when every public school was still, in some sense, a seminary of the Christian religion; when the New Testament was regularly read, every morning, verse about, by all the pupils who could read, and prayer was offered by the teacher. From most of our public schools, if not from all of them, these devout forms have now wholly disappeared, and there is no semblance of religious observance. I do not care to go into the causes of this; perhaps, under existing circumstances, it was inevitable. The perpetuation of mere forms of worship, which do not represent any worshipful feeling, is not a thing to be striven for. The Bible in the schools in the hands of men and women who love the Bible and desire to convey the spirit of its teachings to the hearts of its pupils would be a blessing indeed; but the Bible in the hands of those who do not believe in it nor obey it would work more injury than benefit to religion.

Upon one thing we may, I think, reasonably insist, not wholly in the interest of religion, but quite as much in the interest of general intelligence. Whatever the moral and spiritual value of the Bible may be, there can be no question that it occupies a place in our literature which makes a fair knowledge of it essential to every educated man, no matter what his faith may be.

The Bible is woven through all our literature; names, words, phrases borrowed from it, allusions to it are found on almost every page; without a good knowledge of it much of what he reads will be unintelligible to the reader; familiarity with the Bible lights up with beautiful significance many a passage which would otherwise be enigmatical. Of course the wider is one's knowledge of books in general, the greater is his pleasure and profit in reading, for other books are quoted and alluded to, but there is no book in our language which has been used in this way one hundredth part as much as has the Bible; and for the purposes of general intelligence it is therefore one hundred times as necessary that one should know the Bible as that he should know any other book. This is the fact upon which educators ought to insist. I think that they are beginning to make their voices heard. The most indignant protests which I have heard concerning the amazing popular ignorance of the Bible have come from professors in colleges, whose reports concerning the lack of Biblical knowledge in the pupils that come to them, even from Christian homes and Sunday-schools, are almost incredible. We have now upon the stage a generation which has grown up without any instruction in the Bible in the public schools, and the depth and breadth of popular ignorance respecting the Bible is something astonishing.

If we compare ourselves with other peoples in this respect, we shall find small reason for self-complacency. Pupils educated in German and Scandinavian schools are apt to know something of the Bible, and in England it would appear that an overwhelming majority of the people desire to have the Bible taught in the public schools. It seems to be assumed that this is a book concerning which children need to know something, since it is the one book which has had more to do than all other books put together with the intellectual and civil life of the whole Western world.

Matthew Arnold was considered by many to be a great heretic; certainly he was far from being a bigoted votary of the Christian religion. For a long time he was a school inspector, and had large opportunities of studying the pupils of the public schools and their needs, and he was an enthusiastic advocate of the study of the Bible in the public schools. It was from the point of view of a lover of literature and culture that he reached this conclusion; he always insisted that familiarity with the best literature was the best education; that there was no better way of broadening the mind and cultivating the higher judgment than by getting acquainted with the best that has been thought and said by the great men of the world. And therefore he wanted the Bible studied in the public schools. "Only one literature there is," he said, — "one great literature, for which the people have had a preparation, — the literature of the Bible. However far they may be from having a complete preparation for it, they have some; and it is the only great literature for which they have any. If poetry, philosophy, and eloquence — if what we call in one word *letters* — are a power and a beneficent, wonder-working power in education, through the Bible only have the people much chance of getting at poetry, philosophy, and eloquence. Chords of power are touched in this way which no other part of the instruction in a public school reaches, and chords various, not the simple religious chord only." And in his report to the Education Department he submits these suggestions to school boards: "Let them make the main outlines of Bible history, and the getting by heart a selection of the finest psalms, the most interesting passages from the historical and prophetical books of the Old Testament and the chief parables, discourses, and exhortations of the New, a part of the regular school work." This counsel has been practically followed by most of the school boards in England. In 1895 there were in England and Wales 2392 school boards, of which there were but 91, and these in very small places, which provided no religious teaching; in the schools of the other 2300 with their two millions of pupils, the Bible is read daily, and some such careful provision as has been described is made for the instruction of the children in this great literature.

It appears to me that something of this nature may yet be hoped for in connection with our public education, and that the subject is one which the Christian ministry ought to keep in sight. Whatever is done must be done with great prudence, and it must be evident that the interests in view are not those of dogmatism, but rather of general intelligence. We study Homer, the Bible of the old pagan Greeks, in our schools, with no objection; doubtless if any one wanted to study the Zendavesta, the religious book of the old Persians, or the Niebelungenlied, the religious book of the Scandinavians, that would be thought innocent, if not laudable; but the proposition to study our own Bible, which, from every point of view, as literature, as history, as philosophy, as moral teaching, is infinitely more important than any or all of these, seems to fill the minds of some people with vague alarms. There seems to be no reason in this, and I hope that by and by we shall get ashamed of it, and bring the Bible back into our schools. To make it the basis of doctrinal teaching would be, of course, impossible; but we might have the occasional reverent reading of it, and we might, at least, teach the pupils to discern the beauty of its poetry and the glory of its eloquence and the uplifting power of its prophetic ideals.

The family is the social unit, and all the forces which are employed in social construction have their norms in the life of the family. One great part of the business of the home is to fit its inmates to bear their part in society, — in the life of the commonwealth. Civilized men live in communities, and the art of living includes the art of living together. The primary school in which this art is learned and practiced is the family. No higher function belongs to the family than that of equipping those who are under its discipline with such an outfit of principles, sentiments, and habits of thought and action as shall enable them to fulfill their duties to the community. This involves the ability to take care of themselves, so that they shall not be a burden on the community. Industrial training, intellectual training, moral training, — all these the children ought to receive in the household. The parents have brought these children into the world, and they are bound to see that the children are fitted to live in the world productively, worthily, and happily. Responsibility for the education of the children rests primarily upon the parents, and can never be shifted without social injury.

We find, however, that the actual work of education is now largely done outside the family. The function of education has been specialized; the school has assumed a large share of the work for which the parents are primarily responsible. This has come about for two reasons.

In the first place, a large number of the parents living in our modern society are incapable of educating their children; for this reason society furnishes the school and makes attendance upon it compulsory. This action is often explained as part of its function of protection. Society is said to be insuring itself against the dangers of ignorance. There are economic reasons also; trained intellects and skilled workers increase the national wealth. And there may surely be ethical reasons, for the training ought to result in better lives and in a more orderly and more peaceful community. Thus society takes the children whose parents are incapable of fulfilling the parental function, and gives them that equipment for good living which they could not hope to receive in their homes. The school is then, in part, intended to supply defects of parental training.

But it is more than this. If there were no ignorant or degraded households, if all parents were intelligent and conscientious, there would still be need of the school, as a specialized educational function, in which the children should receive instruction from men and women who, because they devote their lives to the work of teaching, are better teachers than most parents could hope to be. Division of labor is useful here as well as in many other departments of life. It is impossible for most parents to have the technical knowledge necessary to teach their children all the different kinds of knowledge which they wish them to acquire. Nor have they always the time necessary to oversee their children's studies. While therefore the parents are primarily responsible for the education of their children, and are bound to see that it is directed to the right ends and conducted in the best manner, they are justified in accepting the assistance which the school affords in securing this result. Most of them, indeed, would be highly culpable if they failed to avail themselves of this important agency for the accomplishment of a purpose which must lie very near their hearts. It is the parent's duty to supply his child with clothing; but it is not any longer his duty to have the clothing spun and woven in his own house; there is a better way of obtaining it. It is his duty to do what he can to preserve the child's health; but it may not always be his duty to administer remedies in sickness; it may be wise for him sometimes to call the doctor. Similarly, it is his duty to attend to the education of his child, and if he is as intelligent as he ought to be, he can do a great deal of that work himself; he ought to be intelligent enough to know whether it is well done; yet it will probably be his duty to send the child to school.

Nevertheless, it must be clearly understood that this is, fundamentally, a parental function; that the school comes in to supplement the home; that its ruling aims must be determined by what is divinest and best in the life of the home; that it must try to do for the children what the wisest and best fathers and mothers desire to do. On the one hand, the parent must see to it that the school is organized and conducted in such a way that it shall carry into effect his highest purposes for his children. He has no right to surrender his children to an agency which is not capable of doing for his children what he wants done for them. It is too true, as a writer in a recent magazine has said, that many a father "comes to think that his son's education, like a suit of clothes, once put into the hands of an artisan of good repute, ceases to be a matter for which he is responsible. A father may not, by gift of staff and scrip, by cries of 'Good luck' and 'God speed,' break the great seal of the paternal bond. A father cannot release himself by putting another in his place. A man shall answer for every act and every omission of the factor to whom he has intrusted his own son. If a son do wrong, if he surrender to low things, if he come to misery, then must the father be condemned."[1] This on the one hand, from the point of view of the home.

On the other hand, the school must be quick to seize this point of view and be directed by it. Not what the actual home or the average home requires of it, but what the ideal home would demand of it, this must be the aim of the school. It must seek to do for the children what the fathers and mothers whose instincts are surest, whose standards are highest, wish to have done. It must try to give to the children who come from the worst homes, and from indifferent homes, the kind of training desired in the best homes.

Nothing short of this could be considered adequate in our estimate of what a school ought

[1] *The Atlantic Monthly*, vol. lxxxvii. p. 69.

to be. We all know that most of our schools, in their administration, fall far below this mark, but none of them can rationally aim at anything lower. And it will be seen at once that, with this for its ruling purpose, the school must take a very high rank among social institutions; that it is invested with a sacred character. Great responsibilities devolve upon it; exalted service is required of it; those who take part in its work ought to be large-minded, pure-minded, high-minded men and women. Sharp, tricky, mercenary, insincere, unscrupulous characters are as much out of place in the school-room as in the pulpit. We cannot always have ideal teachers, any more than ideal preachers; but character is quite as essential in the one calling as in the other.

Moreover it is plain that the essential qualification of the ideal teacher must be a genuine affection. The intellectual equipment is a matter of course; I need not insist on that; that is of the rudiments. The deeper need is the same feeling toward these pupils that the best and wisest parents have for them; the discernment which only love can give of their needs, their deficiencies, their powers, their perils; a strong wish to give them the restraint, the encouragement, the guidance, the stimulus they need, — to enable them to realize themselves. The ideal teacher must therefore be a genuine philanthropist, a lover of his kind, one to whom nothing is so interesting as human character. He must be full of what we ought to mean when we use that hackneyed religious phrase, "love of souls." For souls, let us keep saying, are just human beings, nothing else; and their wonderful endowments, prerogatives, capabilities, are worthy of the enthusiastic devotion of a man or of an angel. To discern the possibilities hidden under the uncouth exterior, the soul of goodness in the turbulent nature; to awaken the dull mind, to steady the wayward will, to lift up the true ideals before generous spirits, — there can be no nobler or more sacred work than this outside of heaven. It is often, no doubt, very discouraging work, almost heart-breaking work, because there is so little response to all these high endeavors. Children come to the school from homes in which no such thoughts are cherished; come with an inheritance of stupidity and indifference to the highest things; come with their minds filled with perverted ideas of life and conduct, and it is hard for the most earnest teacher to gain any influence over them. As Dr. Stanley Hall has told us, we shall never have the ideal school until we have the ideal home. And when the teacher tries to lift up the standard of the ideal home before children who come

PUBLIC EDUCATION 185

from homes that are far below the ideal, the task is often discouraging. But this is the nature of the work to be done, and this is the spirit in which it ought to be done. The school fulfills its true function when it is animated by this purpose. The school has inherited the highest function of the home, and the law of the school must therefore be the law of the home, which is the law of love. Underneath all the intellectual qualifications and the pedagogical preparations must lie the enthusiasm of humanity in its highest form, the deep and genuine desire to help these boys and girls to win a worthy and beautiful manhood and womanhood.

Let no one imagine that this is any Utopian suggestion. No one who knows many teachers will entertain such an idea. There are, indeed, many persons in the teaching profession who come far short of this, but there are not a few whose aim is nothing lower than this; whose work, as they understand it, is the kind of work which I have tried to describe. Teachers of this quality were mine — more than one of them; I shall never repay the debt I owe them. Such teachers have taught my children; for unselfish devotion to their highest interests, for coöperation with my own best efforts for them, I am deeply indebted to some of the men and women under whose influence my children have come in the school-room. And I think I am not mistaken in my impression that this conception of the seriousness and sacredness of the teacher's work is becoming more and more prevalent. In recent conventions of teachers which I have had the privilege of attending, this note has often been struck, and the response to it has been surprisingly prompt and emphatic.

If, then, the ideal school inherits the highest function of the home, what must it undertake to do for the children intrusted to it? What must be its specific aims? We may sum them up in two propositions: —

1. The school must aid the pupil to realize himself, to become what he was meant to be.

2. The school must teach the pupil how to live with others, how to identify his own interests with the interests of his fellows.

These two purposes can never be separated in life, for neither can be accomplished without the other, but it may be well to consider them separately.

1. The school must recognize the value of the individual, and must seek to develop the child along the lines of his highest endowment, in such a way that he shall become a complete and full-rounded personality. There is danger of uniform patterns in education, of trying to

run all minds in one mould. That must be avoided. Wise teachers always try to avoid it. Every boy must be himself, and every girl herself; the Creator's image and superscription stamped on this nature must not be obliterated. This is not saying that faults may not be corrected or weaknesses removed by discipline; the faults and the weaknesses are no part of the divine plan for this life. It is what God means this pupil to become that we are to fix our thoughts upon and help him to attain. The point I am insisting on is that the character which the school must seek to develop is a whole, round, complete character, — a human integer; not a social cipher, but a significant figure; a person capable of self-direction and self-maintenance. Of one thing we must make ourselves sure, that the individual comes to his own and holds his own, in all our social mutations. A commonwealth of nobodies must come to nothing, no matter how benevolent its social programme may be. Therefore all our discipline of education must brace the pupil to stand on his own feet, do his own thinking, conquer his own difficulties, work out his own salvation. The love of the teacher for the pupil must not be the weak indulgence of the overfond parent, who releases the child from responsibility and duty, from struggle and effort, but the clear firmness of the wise parent who holds the child steadily to his work and helps him to win such a mastery of his powers as shall make him the lord of circumstance and not its slave.

I am thinking, when I say this, of the school as a social institution, and of its great business of preparing these boys and girls to take their place and do their work in the social order. For the secure foundation of democratic society must be men and women who are not fractions but integers; who can think and judge for themselves. "Democratic government," says a late writer, "is the standing together of a multitude of men who could each stand alone. Its business is to balk the mob of the fraudulent gains of a sordid good fellowship and to brace them to moral independence. As the scheme of the creation is the integrating of free souls out of the soul of God, and as God thrusts forth his child and veils his own face with ever thicker veils, waiting with infinite restraint for the man to act from within himself in original love, so democratic government must reflect the austerity of God; must break up the solidarity of passion and pelf to the ends of unanimity, — the voluntary coöperation of free persons."[1] To develop this free personality in the pupil is the first great business of the school.

[1] *The Religion of Democracy*, p. 103.

2. But the other purpose of teaching the pupil to live with others, — of inspiring him with social sentiments and social aims — is inseparably connected with this. The school must teach the pupil to love himself enough to realize himself, to become what God meant him to be, and it must also teach him to love his neighbor as himself. With all his gettings, the pupil ought to get from the school the understanding of this great truth that we are members one of another, and must be helpers one of another; that we must not look upon our own things exclusively, but also on the things of others; that duties are more fundamental than rights in the perfect social order. The whole life of the school ought to express this genuine fraternity. It is one great task of the family to socialize its members, to fill them with the sentiments and drill them in the habits which shall fit them to take their place in a Christianized society. The school, as the inheritor of the work of the home, has the same work to do.

In speaking not long ago of the motives appealed to in the school-room, I said that the competitive spirit was largely relied upon to secure good work. A teacher, whose knowledge of present methods is better than mine, thought my statement too strong, and expressed the opinion that such motives are not now greatly relied on, and that such appeals have been to a great extent abandoned. I have no doubt this is true, in many of the best schools. But the conditions to which I referred must still exist, to a considerable extent, for I find John Dewey, professor of Pedagogy in the University of Chicago, saying this in a recent publication: —

"In the school-room the motive and the cement of social organization are alike wanting. Upon the ethical side the tragic weakness of the present school is that it endeavors to prepare future members of the social order in a medium in which the conditions of the social spirit are eminently wanting. . . . The mere absorption of facts and truths is so exclusively individual an affair that it tends very naturally to pass into selfishness. There is no obvious social motive for the acquirement of mere learning, there is no clear social gain in success thereat. Indeed, almost the only measure of success is a competitive one, in the bad sense of that term — a comparison of results in the recitation or in the examination, to see which child has succeeded in getting ahead of others in storing up, in accumulating the maximum of information."[1]

Just how this can be avoided I do not know, nor am I sure that it is altogether evil; but there is plainly a tendency here which needs to

[1] *The School and Society*, pp. 28, 29.

be well watched, and a great need of finding some adequate means of awaking and cultivating that feeling of identity of interest, that social sympathy, which is the only bond of peaceful and stable society. Professor Dewey thinks that he finds such a corrective to the egoistic tendencies of school life in the industrial training which is finding place in some of our school systems. Doubtless most of us have considered that to be mainly intended to fit the pupil to take care of himself, and it certainly has a valuable work to do in that direction, but Professor Dewey's observation points out its socializing tendency: —

"The difference," he says, "that appears when *occupations* are made the articulating centres of school life is not easy to describe in words; it is a difference in motive, of spirit, and atmosphere. As one enters a workshop in which a group of children are actively engaged in the preparation of food, the psychological difference, the change from more or less passive and inert recipiency and restraint to one of buoyant, outgoing energy is so obvious as fairly to strike one in the face. Indeed, to those whose image of the school is rigidly set, the change is sure to give a shock. But the change in the social attitude is equally marked. . . . When the school work consists in simply learning lessons, mutual assistance, instead of being the most natural form of coöperation and association, becomes a clandestine effort to relieve one's neighbor of his proper duties. When active work is going on, all this is changed. Helping others, instead of being a form of charity which impoverishes the recipient, is simply an aid in setting free the powers and furthering the impulse of the one helped. A spirit of free communication, of interchange of ideas, suggestions, results, both successes and failures of previous experiences, becomes the dominating note of the recitation. So far as emulation enters in, it is in the comparison of individuals, not with regard to the quantity of information personally absorbed, but with regard to the quality of the work done — the genuine community standard of value. In an informal but all the more pervasive way the school life organizes itself on a social basis." [1]

Whatever may be said of the value of the particular method suggested by Professor Dewey, the result which he reports is the thing to be aimed at. Somehow the school must find a way to cultivate the social temper, the habit of coöperation, the spirit of service, the consciousness of fraternity. The fact that we live together in the community, not to get out of it all

[1] *The School and Society*, pp. 28–30.

that we can, but to give all we can of unselfish ministry to one another and to the common welfare, is the truth that should somehow be made fundamental in the teaching of the school.

It must be evident to all who will reflect upon it that the school can never fulfill its true function until it clearly sets before itself this great aim of socializing the pupil. Merely to sharpen intellects and discipline powers that may be used in pushing and fighting, in grasping and holding fast, is not the true work of the school; it must make men and women of these boys and girls, men and women who can stand alone; but they must be men and women who stand to serve, not to strive; to help, not to hurt; to lift up the fallen, and not to trample on the weak.

It is a great and beautiful service to which the school calls men and women. How high and sacred it is, many of us do not realize. If we did, we should be more careful about the choice of those to whom these great interests are intrusted, and we should guard with vigilance the portals of the temples where this priesthood of learning performs its ministry, lest anything that worketh harm or shame should enter therein. And I know not where the responsibility for this guardianship rests more heavily than on the Christian ministry. If the function of the public school is what we have seen it to be, then its work is essentially the same as that of the church. To build character and to strengthen the social bond is its high calling, and to work like this the Christian minister cannot be indifferent. If there is any danger that the school will be turned away from this high aim, he is the man above all others who ought to be vigilant to avert that danger. It is for him, more than any other man in the community, to see that the ideals which guide in public education be kept high and true. The interests for which the public schools, when rightly guided, are working, are the interests to which he has consecrated his life. The methods of the church differ somewhat from the methods of the school, and the minister is not called to impose his theology or his ecclesiasticism upon the school administration; but he ought to be broad-minded enough to see that the high purpose of the school is one to which he can give a vigorous support; and that he is bound, as a public teacher, to contribute what he can of light and leading to this great enterprise. His right to take an active interest in public education will be conceded.

The Christian minister is likely to find the public school teachers of his neighborhood people well worth knowing. They are not all perfect, any more than the ministers themselves;

but there is no class among our citizens whose aims, on the whole, are higher, or whose work is done in a better spirit. Many of these teachers will be members of your churches, and you will find them among the most devoted and the most useful of your helpers. And you will constantly be encouraged to find how steadily and patiently many of them are endeavoring, in their daily work, to lead the children under their care in the ways of life. With the teachers of his vicinage, the minister ought to be on the best of terms. To support their true aims, to confirm their highest purposes, to give them what cheer and courage and inspiration he can in their difficult work, is one of his high privileges.

He will find, also, as he becomes familiar with the life of the schools, that there is great and constant need of lifting up the thoughts of the people concerning the nature of the work they have to do. There is a constant tendency to lower the standards of public education; to put the emphasis of our demand upon that which is lowest in its work instead of that which is highest; to value the school as an economic rather than a social force. An education, in the view of the great majority of parents, is simply an equipment for gaining a livelihood. That end is not to be despised, but it is not the highest, for the life is more than food and the body than raiment. The utilitarian side of education must be considered, and provided for; the movements in the direction of manual training are laudable; nevertheless, even in these, a true insight chiefly rejoices because of the gains which they will bring to character. The mechanical and domestic training which are thus offered will be mainly useful in helping our boys and girls to see the dignity of productive labor, and in turning their thoughts away from the crowded paths of trade and speculation.

One of the great difficulties with which earnest teachers have to contend is the coarse and low philosophy of life which many of the children bring with them from their homes; which makes them blind to the uses of any study that does not seem to contribute directly to some form of money-making; and which leaves wholly out of sight the value of the knowledge by which their life is broadened, their tastes are refined, their ideals exalted, and their power to serve their generation increased. One great reason why our life is so sordid, — why so many men pour out all their energies in money-grubbing, is that our people are so poorly educated that they do not know how else to find enjoyment. The higher pleasures of life have no meaning for them.

PUBLIC EDUCATION

Doubtless education is more generally diffused in America than in any other country; but one is rather startled to find how limited are the educational attainments of the average American. A computation recently made by the United States Commissioner of Education shows that up to 1900, the average American had received 998 days' schooling; which means five school years, of forty weeks. "This estimate includes instruction in the common schools, and also in private schools and colleges."[1] The computation indicates a wonderful gain, since it was estimated that up to 1800, the total schooling enjoyed by the average American had been only 82 days. During the century the amount of education imparted to each citizen had been multiplied twelve-fold. But five years of schooling is not enough to give a human being an adequate equipment for the life of this time. It is somewhat disquieting to know that the education of the average man and woman stops with the fifth grade of the primary school. One reason of this is the wholly inadequate idea, in the minds of the parents, of what education is for; the notion that its significance is summed up in breadwinning; the failure to see that to live is something

[1] *Report of Commissioner of Education*, 1899–1900, vol. i. p. xvi.

more than to get a living. To a popular journal asking the question, "Does a college education pay?" President Hyde gave this answer: "To be at home in all lands and all ages; to count nature a familiar acquaintance, and art an intimate friend; to gain a standard for the appreciation of other men's work and the criticism of one's own; to carry the keys of the world's library in one's pocket, and feel its resources behind one in whatever task he undertakes; to make hosts of friends among the men of one's own age who are to be the leaders in all walks of life; to lose one's self in generous enthusiasm and coöperate with others for common ends; to learn manners from students who are gentlemen and form character from professors who are Christians — these are the returns of a college for the best four years of one's life."[1] One can imagine Mr. Gradgrind rubbing his eyes over that reply. The meaning of it would be far from him. Yet this is the real value of a college education, and all education is precious in proportion as it leads the pupil along this road, and opens his mind and his heart to the real significance of the life he is living, to the beauty and wonder of the world about him. The chief end of education is to put the man into harmony with his environ-

[1] *The Forum*, vol. xxxii. pp. 561, 562.

ment, not merely industrial, but natural and social and spiritual; to open the windows of his soul that the light of the universe may shine in; to fit him to stand in his lot, and receive his portion, and do his work as one of the sons of God. If the boys and girls of your congregation, and their fathers and mothers too, do not get from you some inkling of these higher meanings of education, your work as ministers will be very imperfectly done.

The weakness of our public school system at the present time is found in the character of the governing boards, by which the schools are controlled. This is not the universal fact. In many of the smaller towns and cities the traditions of the earlier periods are in force, and men are selected to govern the schools who have some fitness both in knowledge and in character for their high trust. In a few of our larger cities, also, serious attempts have been made to put the management into capable hands. But it is true of a great many communities that the men chosen by the people for this most difficult service are, for the most part, men who are utterly destitute of the intelligence and the experience which the service requires. The schools have been dragged into party politics, and the ward bosses dictate the nomination of members of the school board. Small politicians in each locality seek the nomination for purposes of their own. There is a little patronage to dispense; janitors and other officers are to be appointed; the politician hopes, by the control of this patronage, to construct for himself a small machine which will be useful in pushing him for some more lucrative position. There are also contracts to let and considerable sums of money to spend; there are school-book publishing companies to deal with whose methods are notorious; and the less scrupulous hope to get something for their votes in important transactions. Such are the influences which guide the selection, in many cases, of the men who control our schools, who manage their important financial operations, who determine upon courses of study, and upon the choice of text-books, who select and instruct the teachers. It is within the truth to say that in a very large number of cases all these great questions are decided by the votes of men who are utterly and brutally ignorant of all the matters with which they are dealing, and who are guided by no higher motive than their own corrupt and sordid interest. It is amazing that the American people should sit still and see this great institution degraded and despoiled after this fashion.

The only reason why the schools in many communities have not been ruined is that the teachers have preserved some sense of the sacredness of their vocation, and have managed to hold up the standards. Whatever of high-mindedness, and honor, and devotion to truth and duty find their way into our schools come, in most cases, from our teachers, and are not the inspiration of the governing boards. In their own associations the teachers cultivate these higher interests; such contact as they have with the school boards is often more apt to lower their aims and blur their convictions than to have any uplifting influence. Observe that I am speaking of what is often true, — of what, I fear, is true in the majority of our larger communities; not of what is universally true. I hope that you may all find your ministry appointed to you in places like my own old home of Springfield, in Massachusetts, where the best men of the community were on the school board, and all the affairs of the schools were guided with the broadest intelligence and the most inspiring wisdom. But if such should not be your happy lot; if, instead, you should find yourselves in communities where the great interests of education are prostituted to the service of ward politics, there will be a call upon you for some faithful testimony and some courageous leadership against a great iniquity. If the function of the public school is what this argument has shown it to be, then it is a monstrous absurdity to leave it in the hands of such men as are now controlling it in a great many American communities.

There are other phases of popular education of which, if there were time, I could find much to say to you. The public libraries and reading-rooms, the university extension lectures, the Chautauqua circles, the educational classes of the Young Men's Christian Association, and the Citizenship Clubs of the Christian Endeavor Societies, all these and many similar institutions and enterprises will enlist your interest, and find in you, I am sure, judicious and efficient support. Your own churches, wherever they may be, will be, I have no doubt, educational institutions of recognized value to the communities in which they stand. You will be preachers of the gospel, that is the first clause in your commission; but you will be teachers also, that is part of your high calling. And you will find ways of making your pulpit minister, week-days and Sundays, to the higher intelligence of the community; of winning for your churches the respect and gratitude of all true children of the light. For this is one of the ways of saving men, — of saving them from the doom of darkened minds and sordid pleasures, and of leading them into communion with God through his works, and into the fellowship of the Spirit in the lives of his children.

VII

THE REDEMPTION OF THE CITY

MANY of you, I trust, will have the good fortune to begin your ministry in country churches. The field of labor which is offered to an enterprising young minister in a rural church appears to me very attractive. The great obstacle to success in these small communities is the appalling number of sects in most of them, among which the Christians are subdivided. Where these morbid conditions are less acute, and any church has a fair chance of uniting the rural community, it would be possible for the right sort of man to do a kind of work for which the city gives a much less attractive opportunity. The thing to be done is to make the church and the minister's house the centre of a kind of social settlement into which the people of the countryside could be gathered into groups of various kinds for study and wholesome diversion and charitable work. The people of the country districts are not apt to be paupers, and there would be few eleemosynary features connected with such a work; but they need social opportunities far more than the people of the slums need them; and I believe that the idea of the social settlement in the city could be adapted to the country districts in a way which would give great vitality to the church and make it the source of boundless benefits to the people in its neighborhood. A young minister and his wife, both of whom were clear-headed and fresh-hearted, with invention, and initiative, and the love of souls, — that is, of men and women and boys and girls, — could go into a community of this kind and work wonders. I lived in the country until I was sixteen years of age, and I know the country people well enough to be sure that they would respond in a very enthusiastic way to such leadership. Clubs of boys and girls could be formed; classes for the study of good literature and of social questions could be organized; debating societies, natural history societies, choral unions, could be tried; the life of the whole neighborhood could be filled with light. The people of the cities do not need these things, and do not care for them half so much as the people of the country would care; the church which undertook in this way to minister to their need would win their enthusiastic loyalty. I suppose that the grange, in many places, does supply this

THE REDEMPTION OF THE CITY

need to some extent; but it is the kind of work that the church ought to do. The deeper spiritual needs of the people should by no means be neglected; the Sunday preaching services should be the central fire from which all this warmth and light should radiate; it should be evident to all that the motive of all this work is a genuine Christly love; it should only be a new revelation of what Christianity is able to do to vitalize and irradiate the whole life of man.

That is all there is, my brethren, of the lecture that should have been written, and that I wanted to write, about the social life of the country church. The subject has greatly interested me, and I wanted to find the time to visit a good many of these country churches, and talk with the pastors and study the conditions on the ground, so that I might speak about it from adequate knowledge. I could not do that, and I am therefore compelled to dismiss it with these rudimentary suggestions. I hope that you will get some one else to take it up who knows all about it, and that many of you will be fortunate enough to work out the problem for yourselves.

But many of you will be called to work in the cities; all of you will find that your lives and your labors are more or less affected by conditions in the cities, for the cities are becoming, more and more, a dominating influence in our whole national life; and it is of the problem of the city that I have promised to speak to you in this concluding lecture.

Of all the social questions confronting us, this seems to me the most difficult, the most urgent, the most portentous. The clear solution of this would greatly tend to the abatement of several of the social evils which we have been considering; for good government in the cities would check the growth of pauperism and restrain the insolence of prostitution and put to flight the armies of the gamblers and compel the liquor-sellers to obey the laws. Most of these evils thrive upon the inefficiency and corruption of our municipal governments.

No one who has lived and labored for many years in ill-governed cities, in the interests of virtue, can fail to be aware of the evil influence which bad government exerts upon the characters of those who live under it. The tone of public morality is affected; the convictions of the youth are blurred; the standards of honor and fidelity are lowered. That which in the family and in the Sunday-school and in the day-school and in the pulpit we are teaching our children to regard as sacred, the bad city government, by the whole tenor of its administra-

THE REDEMPTION OF THE CITY 207

tion, openly despises; the things which we tell them are detestable and infamous, the bad city government, by its open connivance or inaction, proclaims to be honorable. The whole weight of the moral influence of a municipal government like that which has existed until recently in New York, like that which exists to-day in Philadelphia, and in many other cities, is hostile to honesty, honor, purity, and decency. The preacher of righteousness finds, therefore, in bad municipal government, one of the deadliest of the evil forces with which he is called to contend. The problem of the city is a problem in which he has a vital interest, a question on which he has an undoubted right to speak.

The American city of the nineteenth century has been notable for two things, the rapidity of its growth and the corruptness of its civic administration. The population of the whole land has been growing apace, but the cities have grown at the expense of the rural districts. There is scarcely a town of five thousand inhabitants, east or west, which lost population within the past fifty years, and there are scores and hundreds of towns which have grown within that time from nothing to tens or hundreds of thousands; while there are many fertile rural districts, east of the Mississippi, of which the population is considerably less to-day than it was fifty years ago. This feature of American life is paralleled in Europe. The cities of the Old World have been growing during the last century almost as rapidly as those of the New, and many of them, also, have grown at the expense of the agricultural districts.

American cities are distinguished also for the dishonesty and inefficiency with which their business is administered. This is not the universal fact; one can point to cities here and there which are thoroughly well governed; but I fear that it is the general fact. Most of these cities are encumbered with enormous debts, — debts which are burdensome to industry and thrift; and for a large portion of these debts the taxpayers have never had and never will have any adequate return. The municipal governments have been used, in many cases, for spoiling the people. To accomplish this, corrupt alliances have been formed by municipal politicians with the disorderly and vicious classes, and a free rein has been given to those malefactors who get their living by corrupting and debauching their fellow men. Worse than this — far worse in every way — are the corrupt alliances which have been made between the city politicians and the managers of quasi-public corporations by which valuable franchises have been obtained for little or nothing, and power to levy tribute upon the community has been granted for years to come. These corrupt relations between quasi-public corporations and city governments are a comparatively recent development in most of our cities. The great value of these franchises has not, until lately, been appreciated by the general public. The builders of street railways, the promoters of gas companies and electric-lighting companies, were regarded as public benefactors, and the public was willing that they should have everything they asked for. But the municipal politicians have found out that they are worth something to them at any rate; and for the last decade they have been reaping freely where they had not sown, and gathering abundantly where they had not strewed.

We are warranted by revelations which have appeared, east and west, in saying that there are millions on millions of dollars in this country, ready to be paid for franchises by which the people may be taxed to enrich the managers of quasi-public corporations. It is generally believed that a great deal of money has been used by such manipulators in electing municipal officers and in debauching them after they were elected. It is largely to this cause that the corrupt character of our present city governments is due. The men who zealously seek municipal offices are apt to be the kind of men who wish to use such opportunities of gain as the corporations afford them. Powerful but silent influences are all the while at work in many communities to secure the nomination and election of men who can be used in this way. And the men who manage the political machinery are often believed to be receiving large contributions from the managers of such corporations, and are thus under obligation to aid them in securing the nomination of men who will be serviceable to them.

We have here one of the more recent and more powerful of the forces at work to produce municipal misrule. But other causes lie deeper.

1. We must admit a considerable debasement of the average intelligence and morality of the urban populations, due to several causes: —

(1) To immigration, which drops its sediment largely in the cities, and leaves in them great masses of people who do not speak the English language, and who can have no conception of the duties of citizenship.

(2) To industrial crises and fluctuations which push multitudes over the borders of self-maintenance into the limbo of irresponsibility and semi-mendicancy.

(3) To the constant influx of ne'er-do-weels from the neighboring country, who prefer to

take their chances of livelihood among the odd jobs and the alms of a city rather than engage in any regular industry.

(4) To a sentimental and undiscriminating charity, which creates an economic demand for beggars and tends to the deterioration of character.

(5) To the abandonment, by the churches, of those districts where their presence is most needed.

(6) To the absenteeism of large numbers who are the natural leaders of the municipality, but who have removed to the suburbs and lost their citizenship in the cities.

To these and doubtless to other causes we may trace a certain degree of debasement in the mental and moral quality of urban citizenship. If, for any reason, the general average of intelligence, thrift, self-reliance, and virtue in any community has been lowered, we shall find in this deterioration a great cause of failure in our municipal governments.

2. Out of such conditions springs the demagogue as naturally and as quickly as the toadstool springs from the compost heap. The demagogue is produced by these conditions, his interest lies in perpetuating them. Action and reaction are equal, and, in this case, in the same direction.

3. The thoroughgoing partisanship of the reputable people is another prime cause of bad government. The great majority of moral and upright citizens can be relied on to vote the regular ticket if Beelzebub is the nominee. This infatuation affects deacons and elders of churches, Sunday-school superintendents, staid professional men, great multitudes of citizens who are on most other subjects tolerably sane. Such being the combination, the disreputable classes, who are never partisans, are, of course, easily masters of the situation. The demagogues, with such following as they can muster, hold the balance of power. The decent people will vote the straight ticket; they need not, then, be considered in making nominations. Fernando Wood once advised "pandering a little to the moral sentiment of the community," but that is not, by the managers, thought to be important. The problem is to present candidates who will be acceptable to the immoral sense of the community.

I have been speaking, in these last sentences, in the present tense, when perhaps I should have spoken in the past. Signs of promise have appeared, here and there, indicating a purpose in some quarters to break the shackles of partisanship. But in reckoning up the causes which have produced the evil conditions now

THE REDEMPTION OF THE CITY

existing, this must be named as one of the most productive.

4. When the misrule begins to be intolerable, the city is fain to flee to the legislature for relief. Some reorganization is proposed, or some statutory contrivance is suggested, by which it is supposed that the mischiefs will be corrected. The citizens are afraid that they cannot cope with the demagogues, and they are all too busy to give much time to municipal affairs, so they beg the legislature to take the job of governing the city off their hands. Having permitted the municipality to fall into this slough, they call on some power above them to come down and pull it out. The interference of the legislature in municipal politics is not apt to be wholly beneficent. It has been discovered, in some of our states, that cities can be reorganized for partisan purposes, and that the municipal patronage can thus be used as a make-weight in state and national elections. Some of the worst evils in our city governments have arisen from this source. So it has come about that seven other devils, let loose from the State House, and worse than the home-bred demagogue, have entered into the City Hall, and the last state of that municipality was worse than the first.

5. What Mr. Charles Francis Adams calls "the disease of localism" is one cause of bad

government. Every American city, so far as I know, is divided into wards; each ward is erected into a petty political principality, and the ward "boss" and the ward "heeler" are thus called into existence. Here is the *nidus* of pestilent politics. The ward, as a political division, calls for the frequent gerrymander, and it opens the city council to the active operations of the log-roller. The member from each ward wants something which none of the members of the other wards would vote for on its merits; but by a combination of interests all these selfish schemes are realized, and their accumulated burden is piled upon the taxpayer. This excess of localism weakens the corporate unity of the municipality; it results, inevitably, in the deterioration of its representatives in the council; the greediness of the precinct is fostered at the expense of municipal pride and patriotism. I quite agree with Mr. Adams that this is one cause of the low condition of municipal politics.

6. Municipal politics follow the lines of national politics, and are thus wholly destitute of meaning. Neither party, in a municipal contest, has any ideas to contend for; nothing is at stake but the possession of the offices. The only principles at stake are John Randolph's famous seven, five loaves and two fishes. Poli-

THE REDEMPTION OF THE CITY 215

tics which rest on such a basis are not likely to rise much above the level of the curbstone.

If such are some of the causes of bad government in our American cities, then it may be possible to indicate some practicable remedies. Let me speak first of certain changes which would, in my judgment, prove helpful in securing better government, — changes of organization and method. I do not put much weight on these; I do not believe that any mere changes of method will accomplish much, unless deeper changes in the character and purpose of the citizens accompany them; but a good method is better than a bad one, and a good workman is sometimes crippled by a poor tool. Some methods of governing cities are better than others, and we are bound to get the best.

First, then, I believe that it would be well to have in the constitution of every state a positive limit upon the power of the legislature to interfere in municipal affairs. The constitution of every state should furnish a few simple rules to which all city charters must conform, and should prescribe the methods by which the citizens of every city, in representative conventions, should frame their own organic law, submitting it, when framed, to popular approval. In some of the newer states this liberty is given, and I regard it as an important step in the direction

of good government. The people of each city
should frame their own charter, as the people
of each state frame their own constitution.
And considerable freedom should be given in
these enabling acts for the construction of the
municipal machinery, that the people of every
community may be permitted to express their
life in their own terms, and that experiments of
various kinds may be tried in various localities.
Thus the right of home rule, in the largest
sense, should be guaranteed to every city, and
it should be made impossible for the citizens to
shirk their responsibility for good government
upon the legislature. If they want bad government,
let them have it, to their hearts' content,
and know that they and nobody else are
to blame for it. Such a measure would result,
as I believe, in greatly strengthening municipal
pride and patriotism. The city corporation
would no longer be a mere creature of the legislature;
it would be the work of the people's
own hands, and they would feel an additional
degree of responsibility for its wise administration.

2. The proposition to restrict the suffrage in
municipalities is frequently heard. The rule
prevailing in English cities appears to be a good
one, — that no one shall vote for city officers
who has not a fixed residence, who cannot

show that he is the occupier of definite premises within the corporation limits. On the other hand, every such occupier of city premises should have the right to vote in city elections whether his domicile be in the city or not. All men, or women either, who own or rent stores or shops or offices which they occupy for business purposes, ought to be permitted to register and vote in municipal elections. They are stockholders in that great corporation which we call the city; they pay taxes, either directly or indirectly; they are immediately and pecuniarily concerned in having clean streets, good sewerage and sanitation, cheap light, pure water, adequate transportation — in every interest which is represented in the city government, and they ought to have a voice in that government. The fact that they live elsewhere, and have a voice in other local governments, is no reason why they should not be permitted to vote in this municipality, any more than a man who is a stockholder in several business corporations should be forbidden to vote in more than one of them. A man should vote for President of the United States or for member of Congress or for state officers in only one place; but there is no reason why he should not vote for municipal officers in the city where he spends his days as well as in the city where he spends his nights.

This is the rule in many of the English cities, and I can think of no principle of law or of political science or of morals with which it is in conflict. Conditions would be materially improved in several American cities, if their business men who reside in the suburbs were permitted to take part in their municipal affairs.

3. The abolition of the ward as a political division and the election of the council and the board of education upon a general ticket appears also to me a measure of some importance. This would involve some plan of proportionate or minority representation, or some form of cumulative voting.

4. The question concerning the centralization of executive power in the hands of the mayor has been warmly debated. The best city governments of which we have knowledge — those of British cities — are governments by council; all the executive work is under the direction of council committees; the mayor has no executive functions. If we could hope to secure, in our American cities, for long terms of years, the services in the council of from forty to one hundred of the ablest and most responsible men in the city, such a system might be trusted to work very successfully. The English municipal system follows the analogy of the English Parliament, and it has been working thus far with

great efficiency. But the conditions in this country are so different that it is doubtful whether the English system could be made to work. It is probable that we shall adhere to our method of separating the executive from the legislative function, and if that is done, it is undoubtedly better to concentrate than to scatter executive responsibility. The recent tendency to give the mayor the power of appointing, without confirmation, and of removing at pleasure the heads of departments is probably wise, in the existing state of public opinion. It has not always resulted in good government; it may give us very bad government indeed, if the people are careless about the choice of mayor; but in such a case bad government is precisely what is deserved, and the worse it is the better. It is only by bringing immediately home to the people the consequences of their carelessness that they will cease to be careless. When they wake up, as they have in New York, and choose a thoroughly upright and capable mayor, the concentration in his hands of executive responsibility will be found to be a great advantage. Does any sane man think that it would be better to have the power now conferred on Mr. Low dispersed among a number of boards or commissions, or shared by him with the municipal council?

5. A rigid civil service system, fairly enforced, with competitive examinations rationally adapted to each department, is also required. It is well to put considerable emphasis on the phrase "fairly enforced." It is sometimes true that civil service laws are enacted by the party which is about to vacate the offices, for the purpose of keeping its own members in office; and experience has proved that such laws can be administered for partisan purposes. On the other hand, an incoming mayor may assume that the men whom he finds in office are all rascals, and may manage to establish the most hostile relations between himself and those employees whom the civil service laws protect against his arbitrary removal. A civil service law will not accomplish much good if it is used to screen incompetent officials, or if the executive authorities hate it and constantly seek to break it down. But a civil service law judicially administered by the commission, and heartily accepted by the executive officers, will result in a great improvement in the public service.

Such, then, are some of the legal changes which seem to me to be desirable in the organization and administration of our municipalities. To give all cities the constitutional right to frame and amend their own charters; to extend the municipal franchise to all persons owning or renting real property in the city, whether living within the corporation limits or not; to abolish the ward, as a political division, and elect councils and boards of education on general tickets; to centralize the executive in the person of the mayor and to put the municipal service on the basis of the merit system, — these measures would, I am persuaded, have some tendency to purify and strengthen municipal governments. Yet I do not put forth this programme as a panacea. I am perfectly well aware that with this machinery all in motion we might have very bad government. Something more than the most improved political machinery is necessary to secure good municipal government. What is necessary?

In the first place the people of the cities must have some conception of what a well-governed city would be. We must have ideals, and keep them steadily before our eyes. The seer in the book of Revelation saw the Holy City, the New Jerusalem, descending out of heaven from God. Mr. Drummond tells us that as John saw in his vision the New Jerusalem, so we must see the New London, the New Boston, the New Chicago, the New New York; the city that ought to be; the regenerated, purified, redeemed city; we must see it, and believe in it, and be ready to work and suffer to bring it down to earth.

Nothing that is worth doing is ever done in this world except under the inspiration of high ideals which take possession of the souls of men and control their conduct. What will that city be which shall occupy the ground where the city now stands which to me is most dear? Let me try to picture it.

It will be a well-governed city, — a city in which law will be respected by the magistrates and obeyed by the citizens, whose streets will be safe by night and by day; a city in which the industries that debauch and degrade men shall not have larger opportunities than those which minister to their welfare; a city in which the strong are not permitted to aggrandize themselves, through legal privilege, at the expense of the weak; a city in which the great coöperative enterprises are economically and efficiently conducted for the public good and the revenues accruing therefrom are carefully expended for the benefit of the whole people. I trust that it will be a city in which the people have learned to coöperate in a great many ways for their own profit, securing for themselves vast benefits, at small cost, through associated effort. I hope that it will be a city in which there will be not only great parks and boulevards on the outskirts, but many small pleasure grounds scattered through the whole area, within easy reach

THE REDEMPTION OF THE CITY

of all the homes. I hope that libraries, reading-rooms, great art galleries, and fine orchestras will provide for the education of all the people, without money and without price. I hope that the whole city will be so clean and healthy that every part of it shall be safe and desirable for residence; that there will be no vast preserves of opulence in which none but the richest could live, and no sinks of squalor and misery in which none but the poorest would live. I hope that there will be no unemployed, rich or poor, in its population; but that the city will find some way of making it certain that no able-bodied human being who is willing to work shall either beg or starve, and that every able-bodied human being who prefers to beg shall either work or starve.

These may seem to be high hopes, but many of them have been in good part realized elsewhere; I think that they are not irrational; that we may confidently look to the coming years to bring in the substance of these great gains.

But who are to do all these things for us? Who will quench the violence of partisanship, bridle monopoly, purge away corruption, banish pauperism, cleanse the slums, organize the coöperation, open the parks, build the art galleries, equip the orchestras? Who will transform the nineteenth century city, with its rotten politics and its wasteful administration and its rank extremes of riotous wealth and groveling poverty, into the well-ordered, thrifty, peaceful community which we have seen in our dreams?

The people, I answer; the people who live in the city; the men and women of the palaces and the tenement houses; the people in the stores and the shops, the banks and the factories, — the people themselves must do it. Really, when you come to think about it, there is nobody else who can be expected to do it. No legions of angels are coming down from heaven to regenerate our cities; the Congress at Washington will not be able to attend to it, nor will it be well for us to put our trust in the legislature at Columbus or at Albany or at Harrisburg or at New Haven, or in any boards or commissions which it can contrive. No help is coming to us from any of these quarters. We are never going to get good government in the cities till the people of the cities give it to us. The one thing to be desired is that the interference of the state government with municipal affairs shall be reduced to a minimum, and that the responsibility of managing their own business shall be brought directly home to the people of every community. The attempt to take the power away from them, to invent all sorts of legislative

THE REDEMPTION OF THE CITY 225

pokes and hopples by which they shall be prevented from exercising their will, must result disastrously.

The truth is that democracy, with universal suffrage, is our dispensation; we are in for it, and we must fight it out along that line; if we are to be saved at all, we must be saved by the people; if we are to be reformed, the reform must spring from the intelligent choice of the people; it must express their wishes; the notion that by some sort of hocus-pocus we can get society reformed without letting the people know it does undoubtedly haunt the brains of some astute political promoters, but it will not work. No; there is no power in a democracy but the power of the people, and it is the people who are going to give us the regenerated city of the twentieth century, if we ever get it. Nor will it be done by the people of the churches and the colleges and the literary clubs and the art associations. It will not be done without them, but they alone can never accomplish it. A democracy in name which is an oligarchy in fact has no power for such tasks as these. The people of New York have begun to realize that there will never be good government in New York until the people of the East Side are just as earnest in their choice of it and just as clear in their understanding of what it means as the people of Murray Hill; the people of Chicago have got to learn — some of them know — that there will never be good government in that city until the people of Halstead Street have substantially the same mind about it as the people of the Drexel Boulevard.

Let us not underrate our problem. These people of the cities — many of them ignorant, depraved, superstitious, unsocial in their tempers and habits; many of them ignorant of the language in which our laws are written, and unable freely to communicate with those who wish to influence them for good; having no conception of government but that of an enemy to be eluded or an unkind providence from which dole may be extorted; and no idea of a vote higher than that of a commodity which can be sold for money, — these are the "powers that be" who must give us good government in our cities, if we are ever to get it. We need not imagine that we are somehow going to organize a power which will fence these people in and hold them down and keep them harmless, — that we shall get good government by suppressing them; that policy will never work. There are too many of them to manage in this way; and so long as we suffer vast multitudes to remain in this condition, so long we shall have corrupt and costly government. The doom of a democracy is to be as bad as its worst classes; if we want to lift up the government of the cities, we must lift up the whole people.

There is a picture in the sixtieth chapter of Isaiah of a regenerated and glorified city; a city whose officers are peace and whose exactors righteousness; whose walls are salvation and whose gates are praise; a city which has risen from misery and shame to splendor and honor. "Whereas," says the Mighty One of Jacob, "thou hast been forsaken and hated, so that no man passed through thee, I will make thee an eternal excellency, a joy of many generations." And the explanation of how it is to come to pass is given in a single sentence: "Thy people also shall be all righteous." That is the only way in which cities ever were redeemed or regenerated.

Most true it is that many things might be done by the people of the more intelligent and fortunate classes by which the emancipation and elevation of the ignorant and degraded classes could be greatly hastened. A considerable part of their degradation is due to the burdens which the prosperous and the strong wantonly or thoughtlessly impose on them. The tribute which these poor people pay for the enrichment of those who hold valuable franchises is very large. Because it is extorted in cents or fractions of cents it escapes notice; but the sum of such extortion, added together at the end of the year, would make the difference, in many a workingman's life, between squalor and decency, — perhaps between life and death. The gigantic inequalities of taxation, of which President Harrison spoke so sternly not long before his death, all work against the poorest. Such wrongs the rich and the strong can remedy, if they will, at once, without asking leave of those who suffer them. If such wrongs were remedied, the task of reaching these multitudes with light and help would be far less formidable. Yet it would still remain true that for the great and beneficent ends which are involved in good city government these multitudes must be enlisted; they must be civilized, educated, inspired with new ideas; new hopes must be kindled in their hearts; new paths must be opened to their thoughts; new wants must be awakened in them; a wholly new conception of what life means must be somehow imparted to them.

The city of the future which we saw in our dream is simply a great community coöperating for the public good, and in order that the coöperation may be effective, the people must know what is good and how to coöperate. And this involves a mighty change in the characters of multitudes of them!

Well, there is no other way to get the good things that we have set our hearts upon. We must teach these people what life means, and what love means; we must bring some regenerating influence to work upon their characters, by which they shall be transformed in the spirit of their mind, and filled with the sentiments and impulses out of which social coöperation naturally springs. In short, they must be Christianized. That is what must somehow be achieved, if our dream is to be realized. For the constructive idea of that coöperative municipality of which we are thinking is the Christian idea, simply that and nothing more; the idea that we are children of a common Father and therefore brothers, in deed and in truth; the idea that we are members one of another; that each must live for all and all for each. Somehow we must manage to get this idea into the minds of all these people, if we want them to help us in building on the earth the kind of city that we have been thinking about. And, doubtless, nobody can succeed, very well, in getting it into other people's heads, unless he has first got it in his own.

This, then, is the thing that I am hoping for — that our communities are really going to be Christianized; that a great many people are coming to see that the Christian law is meant to live by, to do business by, to rule politics, to organize municipalities upon, and that they are going to make the world believe it. Such a faith as that would have tremendous power over the people in the slums and the tenement houses, to lift them up and make men of them. Before such a faith as that, transforming society, rotten politics and grinding monopolies would shrivel and disappear; under its banner light and beauty, peace and plenty, joy and gladness would be led in.

It is a glorious hope. Have we any reasons for it? We have good and strong reasons.

In the first place, my own confidence goes down to the bedrock of all my beliefs that what ought to be is going to be. If I believe in God at all, I must believe that. Because I am sure that the kind of city we have been thinking about is the kind that ought to exist upon this continent, I am confident that it will exist.

In the second place, I can see signs that it is coming. The last years of the nineteenth century witnessed a great awakening of thought and conscience upon this subject, and the whole trend of opinion is toward the idea that the future city must be a coöperative community. This means that it must be a Christian community; that the people must learn the Christian law, and live by it in all their municipal administration.

But the first thing, as we have seen, is not the machinery, but the motive power; not the forms of a coöperative commonwealth, but the spirit of coöperation, the spirit of social service. It will come when there are enough men and women who are able to put the common welfare above personal gain or pleasure, and to work for the common good with the same self-effacing devotion as that which sends soldiers into the ranks in war-time, missionaries to the African jungles. There is no call to heroic, consecrated service clearer or more imperative than that which summons faithful men and women to give their lives to the service of the cities in which they live. The Master whom we serve has need of loyal representatives and followers in many fields; he needs them on the bloodstained soil of the Flowery Kingdom; he needs them in the famine-stricken lands of India; he needs them in the frontier settlements of the West, and in the cotton-fields and the highland fastnesses of the South, but there is no place where he needs them more, no place where the opportunity of a self-denying devotion is greater, than in the cities of this land, — in taking up the burdens of civic responsibility, in witnessing and working and suffering to redeem the cities from the thralldom of greed and vice and corruption.

It is the men and women who sit every Sunday morning in the pews of our city churches to whom this call comes first and loudest. They, more than any others, are responsible for the redemption of the cities. The cities are in the melancholy condition in which we now find them because they have worn too loosely the bonds of civic obligation. They have been too willing to take from the commonwealth the protection, the privilege, the bounty which it dispenses, and to render little or no return in faithful service. When the city has summoned them to labor and sacrifice they have answered, "I pray thee, have me excused." They have even marveled, sometimes, at the unreasonableness of those who suggested that a man might be required to neglect his business, or to forego some portion of his gains, in order that he might serve the city. That has seemed to them an exorbitant demand. All such estimates of life must be revised. We shall never have good government in our cities till the people who profess and call themselves Christians get some idea of what Christian consecration means, and understand more perfectly what is the high calling of God to the American citizen.

A great part of the inspiring work committed to your hands, my brethren, is to awaken and foster the sentiment of community, the spirit of fraternity, the feeling that business of citizenship is a high and sacred function. There may be some who would doubt the wisdom of socializing, to any greater extent, the mechanism of the state, but there can be none who will question the immense importance of socializing the individual, — of teaching every man in society to think and speak and act with the welfare of the community continually in view. The best part of this work will be done in unofficial and homely ways; by such agencies as the college settlements and the neighborhood guilds which have borne such abundant fruit in the late overturning in New York city; above all by such churches as have comprehended their mission and are devoting themselves to Christianizing the society in which they live. For that kingdom of heaven whose foundation principles are, "No man liveth unto himself," "Ye are members one of another," must in some good degree prevail before our cities will be delivered from that bondage of corruption under which they now groan and travail together. But every word of clear testimony, every act of good-will, every unselfish effort to promote the common weal, helps to bring a little nearer the day of that deliverance.

If, while you are striving after this, some one should admonish you that your business is the saving of souls, it might be well to raise the question how and where it is in this generation that souls are lost. How many of the youth are seduced from the ways of virtue by snares spread in their path through the connivance of weak and corrupt municipal governments? How many citizens find their standards of honesty and honor constantly lowered through the financial rascality which bad city government makes epidemic? Is there any association in which a man loses manhood more rapidly than in the pestilent politics of a rotten municipality? And how about these good people in the pews? Are they running no risks of losing their souls? Is the man in no peril who deliberately spurns the sacred obligations of citizenship because he is unwilling to disturb his leisure or lessen his gains? Are there any who are exposed to deadlier danger than those sleek and comfortable citizens who have handed over the business of governing the cities to the ward bosses and the promoters of monopoly, and who now content themselves with making money and having a good time, while the city goes at a plunging pace to pandemonium? Let us not neglect the business of saving souls; but let us try to get clear ideas of how it is that souls are lost and of what salvation means.

Is there power in the gospel we preach to quicken men's consciences with respect to these highest and most stringent obligations: to convict them of sin when such duties are evaded or denied, and to lead them into a genuine repentance? That is a question which ought to be considered very seriously by every Christian minister. Reflection upon it may lead to the conviction that the saving of souls is a business larger and more urgent than many of those who use the phrase are apt to think.

It is a high calling, my brethren; I give you joy that you have chosen it. There has never been a day, since the Apostolic Band received their first commission, when the work meant so much as it means to-day; when its field was so wide, its opportunities so fair, its promise so inspiring. May God help you to understand all that it means, and to do it, while your day lasts, with all your might!

REFERENCES AND SUGGESTIONS

FOR CHAPTER I

Sociology, by John Bascom.

Jesus Christ and the Social Question, by Francis G. Peabody.

Outlines of Social Theology, and *God's Education of Man*, by William De Witt Hyde.

Social Morality, by Frederic D. Maurice.

Christianity and Social Problems, by Lyman Abbott.

Unto this Last, and *The Crown of Wild Olive*, by John Ruskin.

Social Aspects of Christianity, by Richard T. Ely.

Faith and Social Service, by George Hodges.

Social Reform and the Church, by John R. Commons.

Moral Evolution, by George Harris.

The Divine Drama, by Granville D. Pike.

FOR CHAPTER II

Labor and Life of the People, by Charles Booth.

Christian and Civic Economy of Large Towns, by Thomas Chalmers.

Practical Socialism, by S. A. Barnett.

Hull House Papers and Maps.

American Charities, by A. G. Warner.

How the Other Half Lives, and *A Ten Years' War*, by Jacob A. Riis.

Dependents, Defectives, and Delinquents, by Charles R. Henderson.

238 REFERENCES AND SUGGESTIONS

The Christian Pastor, by Washington Gladden, pp. 448–475.

Reports of International Congress of Charities and Correction, 1893.

FOR CHAPTER III

The Unemployed, by C. Drage.

Problems of Poverty, by J. Hobson.

Massachusetts Report on the Unemployed (1895), by Davis R. Dewey.

The Workers, vols. i. and ii., by Walter A. Wyckoff.

Tramping with Tramps, by Josiah Flynt.

Report on Labor Colonies (in Germany), by J. Mavor.

The City Wilderness, edited by Robert A. Woods.

The Public Treatment of Pauperism, edited by John H. Finley.

Report of Citizens' Relief Committee of Boston, for 1893–94.

The Future Problem of Charity and the Unemployed, by John Graham Brooks, Annals of the American Academy, vol. v. p. 1.

FOR CHAPTER IV

Punishment and Reformation, by F. H. Wines.

Prisons and Child Saving Institutions, by E. C. Wines.

Prisoners and Paupers, by H. M. Boies.

Heredity and Christian Problems, by A. H. Bradford.

History of the Criminal Law of England, by Sir James Stephen.

Crime and its Causes, by William Douglas Morrison.

Dependents, Defectives, and Delinquents, by Charles R. Henderson.

Reports of International Congress of Charities and Correction, 1893.

REFERENCES AND SUGGESTIONS

FOR CHAPTER V

Prohibition, Regulation, and Licensing of Vice, by Sheldon Amos.
Prostitution Considered, by W. Acton.
Fifth Report of the United States Commissioner of Labor.
A State Iniquity, by Benjamin Scott.
The Study of Sociology, by Herbert Spencer, p. 306.
Wealth and Moral Law, by E. B. Andrews.
Applied Christianity, by Washington Gladden, pp. 197–209.
Elements of Ethics, by Noah K. Davis, p. 73.
Economic Aspects of the Liquor Problem, by J. Koren.
The Liquor Problem in its Legislative Aspects, by F. H. Wines and J. Koren.
Substitutes for the Saloon, by Raymond H. Calkins.
Methods of Social Reform, by W. S. Jevons, pp. 236–276.
The Workers, by W. A. Wyckoff.
The Temperance Problem, Past and Future, by E. R. L. Gould, Forum, November, 1894.
Popular Control of the Liquor Traffic, by E. R. L. Gould.

FOR CHAPTER VI

Democracy and Empire, by F. H. Giddings.
Relation of State to Education in England and America; Annals of American Academy, vol. iii. pp. 669–690.
American Contributions to Civilization, by Charles W. Eliot, pp. 203–233.
The School and Society, by John Dewey.
Social Theory, by John Bascom, pp. 351–363.
Education in its Relation to Manual Industry, by Arthur MacArthur.

240 REFERENCES AND SUGGESTIONS

FOR CHAPTER VII

Municipal Government in Great Britain, and *Municipal Government in Continental Europe*, by Albert Shaw.

Reports of Conferences of the National Municipal League for Good City Government, 1894–1900.

Municipal Reform Movements in the United States, by A. H. Tolman.

The City and the People, by Frank Parsons.

Municipal Monopolies, edited by E. W. Bemis.

The Cosmopolis City Club, by Washington Gladden.

Social Facts and Forces, by Washington Gladden, pp. 155–191.

www.ingramcontent.com/pod-product-compliance
Lightning Source LLC
Chambersburg PA
CBHW050138170426
43197CB00011B/1884